DON'T
ASK
YOUR
WAITER

DON'T ASK YOUR WAITER

by
PAULINE WASSERMAN
with
SHELDON WASSERMAN

STEIN AND DAY/*Publishers*/New York

First published in the United States of America
Copyright © 1978 by Pauline and Sheldon Wasserman
All rights reserved
Designed by Ed Kaplin
Printed in the United States of America
Stein and Day/*Publishers*/Scarborough House,
Briarcliff Manor, N.Y. 10510

Library of Congress Cataloging in Publication Data

Wasserman, Pauline.
   Don't ask your waiter.

   1. Food—Dictionaries.   2.   Cookery—
Dictionaries.   I.   Wasserman, Sheldon, joint
author.   II.   Title.
TX349.W37   641.3′003   77-23434
ISBN 0-8128-2243-9
ISBN 0-8128-2244-7 pbk.

to Louis Daniel
one of the finest restaurateurs
we've had the pleasure of knowing

Acknowledgments

We would like to express our appreciation to all those who've offered us helpful suggestions and valuable information and encouragement while we were working on this book.

Especially to Art Ballant, for his enthusiasm for the project and very valuable assistance in turning it from a manuscript into a book, as well as his helpful suggestions.

To Bettina Bien Greaves, for providing very useful and valuable reference materials.

To Lucio Sorré, for his helpful suggestions and useful information.

To Stella Smith for her help with the Russian.

To Roberto Ferin, for suggesting *Don't Ask Your Waiter* as the title for the book.

To André Brunel, for providing some interesting information.

To Harry Foulds, for the encouragement and useful information.

To Peter Buchband, for his helpful suggestions.

To Emanuel Greenberg, for his good advice.

To Patricia Day, for her helpful comments and suggestions of improvements to the manuscript.

Contents

HOW TO USE THIS GUIDE   1
  Key to Pronunciation   4

ON THE MENU   6

ON THE CHEESE TRAY   133

DON'T ASK YOUR SOMMELIER   165

WINE-FOOD AFFINITIES   169

CROSS-REFERENCE   198
  Cheese   198
  Eggs   198
  Game   199
    Hare   199
    Partridge   199
    Pheasant   199
    Pigeon   200
    Quail   200
    Rabbit   200
    Venison   200
  Meat   201

Beef	202
Ham	204
Lamb	204
Mutton	205
Pork	205
Sausages	206
Veal	206
Poultry	207
Capon	208
Chicken	208
Duck, Duckling	209
Goose	210
Turkey	210
Seafood	210
Fish	211
Frogs' Legs	211
Herring	212
Mackerel	212
Salmon	212
Sole	212
Trout	213
Shellfish	213
Clams	214
Crabs	214
Lobster, Rock Lobster	215
Mussels	215
Oysters	215
Scallops	216
Shrimp	216
Snails	216

How to Use This Guide

Dining out in restaurants featuring foods from foreign lands can be a delicious adventure. But it can also be a problem if you don't understand the language on the menu.

Who wants to have to ask the waiter what item after item on the menu is, how it is prepared, with what other ingredients—even assuming he has the information at his fingertips, or the patience to go into term after term with you?

And it's not just foreign words either. English terms can bring up question marks too. How is Steak Diane prepared? What are Sweetbreads? Or Cape Cods?

It would be a shame to miss out on a dish you would love if you only knew what it was, but you don't want to take a chance on a dish that turns out to be your least favorite food either.

What to do?

Don't ask your waiter. The answers are here. Simply look up the unfamiliar menu term in the main listing of this guide. If it's a cheese, there's a separate section for cheeses directly following the main list. And following that, a guide for matching food and wine, with some tips on ordering wine in restaurants. Then there's the cross-reference.

In case you happen to be in the mood for a particular type of meat or seafood—your tastebuds are all primed for a nice piece of beef, say, and the menu is not in English—the cross-reference lists the different types of meat and seafood followed by the name in other languages, then lists preparations commonly used for that type of meat or seafood.

If you come across a term within a definition that you're not familiar with, check it out also in the listing.

The menu terms are listed in alphabetical order. That seems simple enough. But where the name for the dish is more than one word, which word should you look up first? Your best bet is to check out the method of preparation first.

Say it's Chicken Cacciatore, for example. You already know what chicken is, right? So you want to find out what Cacciatore means. But even if it's Pollo alla Cacciatore, you're still better off looking first under the style of preparation (generally the word after "alla" or "à la," or the last word in the name). In many cases this will save you from looking in two different places. Under Cacciatore you find how dishes done hunter-style are prepared, including Pollo (which you find is chicken) alla Cacciatore.

Sometimes the name of the meat (vegetable or whatever) being prepared in a particular style won't be found under the preparation—if it's not a predictable combination, for example. If the restaurant decides to do Bue, say, instead of Pollo, Cacciatore style, then you will have to look up Bue, after having found out what Cacciatore means, if you don't know already that Bue is beef.

It may happen that, despite all our efforts, the dish as made in a particular restaurant doesn't match the definition in the guide. We have tried to give an indication of the kinds of variations usually made, but occasionally the chef doesn't go by the classic or traditional recipe, or even the general interpretation of a dish or a reasonable facsimile thereof. (There's no accounting for a chef in a flight of fancy!) He gives you his own version. And there's always a restaurant that will offer its own twist.

In these cases, though, the menu term is often qualified—or should be—by adding the chef's name (Hasenpfeffer Fritzi) or the name of the restaurant (Moussaka Trojan Horse) to the name of the dish.

This happens less often in French restaurants. There, you can be pretty sure of getting the dish described. French cuisine has to a large extent been classified, the classic recipes written down, and chefs are in agreement that if they're preparing Escargots de Bourgogne, for example, the snails will be done with garlic butter, and that's that—no fooling around.

With the cooking of other countries this is not always the case. Some well-known recipes are made in virtually the same way everywhere they're served, but there are many more that are not.

Which kinds of meat and shellfish will be in a Paella? And what can you expect to come across in a Goulash?

Some dishes are subject to much variation, no question about it, but still there are certain general rules to their preparation—even in Italy, which at first seems to defy classification, for each town has its own way of preparing each particular dish. A dish done this way in this part of the country, is done that way in that. In general, though, the cooking in the north tends to be simpler and more delicate; the dishes of the south, spicier and less sophisticated (but not necessarily any less delicious).

When you get right down to it, many Italian dishes are made in pretty much the same way from ristorante to trattoria, and the variations are not major. This is especially so in Italian restaurants in America.

In looking up a particular term spelling may sometimes be a problem. In cases where a couple of different spellings are frequently used for a dish, we have listed both.

You may, though, come across some exotic variations we haven't been able to anticipate. In this case, you will be called upon to use your imagination. At any rate, it shouldn't happen often.

Sometimes in words with double letters, one has been dropped; sometimes one has been added to make the double, as in Arrugula, Arugula. Some of these spellings have been anticipated.

Singular and plural forms, of course, have different spelling—Osso Buco, Ossi Buchi.

And masculine and feminine gender changes the endings of adjectives: mista, misto, misti—they all mean mixed. But these shouldn't present much of a problem; you'll catch onto them in a jiffy.

For each word that isn't perfectly obvious (as most English words), the pronunciation is given. The chart below explains the letters used for indicating the particular sounds. We've tried to come as close as possible to the correct pronunciation. Certain foreign sounds are very difficult to indicate in writing, but as we can't make the sounds for you to hear, we've done our best with the letters we have.

You won't be speaking like a native, but you should be understood by your waiter. And you won't have to pass up a delicious dish because you don't want to point to the menu and mumble.

Key to Pronunciation

A—a sound between the A in at and the A in father
AH—as in father, palm
AW—as in block, taught

AE—as in tr*ai*t, fl*a*ke; a pure A that doesn't flow into an E sound at the end as in English

E—as in t*e*ll, br*ea*d
EW—not a sound used in English; position the mouth for an OO sound, but say EE
EE—as in f*ee*t, bl*ea*t

I*I*—as in m*i*ne, qu*i*te
IH—as in it, t*i*ll

OH—as in g*o*, h*o*pe
OO—as in t*u*ne, f*oo*d
OW—as in h*ow*, l*ou*d

U—as in *a*lone, *u*p
UH—as in h*e*r, bl*u*r; but without the R sound of those words

Y—as in *y*es; never as an E sound

ZH—as in lei*s*ure, mira*g*e

N or n—a nasal sound, but not quite an N

CAPITAL LETTERS indicate the syllable that gets the emphasis.

On the Menu

À L', À LA (al, a la) *Fr.* In the style of.

ABBACCHIO (ahb-BAHK-kyoh) *It.* Milk-fed, baby lamb.

ABRICOT (a-bree-KOH) *Fr.* Apricot.

ACCIUGHE (ah-CHOO-gae) *It.* Anchovies; their name in northern Italy.

AFFOGATI (ahf-foh-GAH-tee) *It.* Literally, drowned; but for our purposes, steamed; or of eggs, poached.

AFFUMATO, AFFUMICATO (ahf-foo-MAH-toh, ahf-foo-mee-KAH-toh) *It.* smoked.

AGLIATA, ALL' (ah-LYAH-tah) *It.* Seasoned with garlic.

AGLIO (AH-lyoh) *It.* Garlic.

AGNEAU (a-NYOH) *Fr.* Lamb.
AGNEAU DE LAIT (duh lae) Milk-fed, baby lamb.

AGNELLO (ah-NYAEL-loh) *It.* Lamb.

AGNÈS SOREL (a-NYAES soh-REL) *Fr.* Garnished with sautéed mushrooms, smoked or pickled tongue, and sometimes truffles; classically served with broth from the meat it accompanies flavored with a little Madeira. Named for the mistress of Charles VII.
OMLETTE AGNÈS SOREL An omelette filled with sliced sautéed mushrooms and chicken purée, served with veal gravy.

AGRODOLCE, IN (een ah-groh-DOHL-chae) *It.* In sour/sweet sauce. Hare, LEPRE (LAE-prae), or rabbit, CONIGLIO (koh-NEE-lyoh), prepared this way is cut into serving pieces and marinated in red wine seasoned with herbs such as thyme, bay leaf, parsley, sage, rosemary, cloves, and black peppercorns. The meat is floured and sautéed in fat or olive oil, and stewed in the marinade, sometimes with bits of ham. The sauce is sweetened with sugar; and often white raisins and pine nuts are added, sometimes also unsweetened chocolate and candied citron peel.

AIL (AH-yu) *Fr.* Garlic.

AILERONS (ael-RAWN) *Fr.* Wings.

ALFREDO, ALL' (ahl-FRAE-doh) *It.* A style of preparing Fettuccine (faet-too-CHEE-nae) which is mixed—often at your table—with butter, grated Parmesan cheese, and usually heavy cream, especially in America. As served at Alfredo alla Scrofa, the restaurant in Rome (Trastevere) where it was created, it is tossed with just butter and grated Parmesan—lots of butter and lots of Parmesan.

ALICE (ah-LEE-chae) *It.* The southern Italian name for anchovies.

ALL', ALLA (ahl, AHL-lah) *It.* In the style of.

ALLIGATOR PEAR Another name for the avocado.

ALMANDINE See Amandes, Aux.

ALOUETTE (a-LWET) *Fr.* Lark.

ALOUETTES SANS TÊTE (sahn taet) Also called Oiseaux Sans Tête, which see.

ALSACIENNE, À L' (al-za-SYEN) *Fr.* In the style of Alsace. This may indicate a garnish of sausages, ham, sauerkraut (choucroute), or boiled potatoes—most probably sauerkraut, but perhaps even foie gras. Or it may mean simply the way the particular dish is prepared in Alsace. The cuisine of this region tends to be hearty, similar to that of Germany just across the river, but with a lighter hand.

AMANDES, AUX (oh za-MAnD) *Fr.* Prepared with almonds, sometimes toasted almonds.

AMANDINE (a-man-DEEN) *Fr.* Same as Aux Amandes, which see.

AMARETTI (ah-mah-RAET-tee) *It.* Italian macaroons, made with egg whites, sugar, and ground almonds, including bitter almonds. Literally, rather bitter, which seems a bit odd as these are little sweets, but it refers to the bitter almonds.

AMATRICIANA, ALL' (ah-mah-tree-CHAH-nah) *It.* A sauce for pasta, generally spaghetti, in the style of the little town of Amatrice, near Rome. This is a light tomato sauce made with olive oil, diced onion, and bacon or salt pork, which is ladled over the pasta and topped with grated Pecorino cheese; Parmesan is often substituted.

AMBASSADEUR (ahn-ba-sa-DUHR) *Fr.* A garnish of artichoke bottoms filled with puréed mushrooms, creamed potatoes, and grated horseradish.

AMÉRICAINE, À L' (a-mae-ree-KAEN) *Fr.* A style of preparing lobster, HOMARD (aw-MAR). It is cut up and sautéed in its shell in olive oil, with shallots, onions, garlic; chopped tomatoes and white wine and/or brandy are added, and it is seasoned with parsley and tarragon, and sometimes a few grains of hot cayenne pepper, and sometimes thickened with lobster coral and butter. Some believe the name to be a corruption of the name Armoricaine, in the style of Armorica (Brittany). but others, notably Waverley Root, note that this is not the style of cooking done in Brittany, and was more likely named for a now vanished Parisian restaurant named "Américain" where this dish was supposed to have been a specialty.

AMONTILLADO (ah-mohn-tee-YAH-doh) *Sp.* A

medium dry Sherry or Montilla.

ANANAS (a-na-NA) *Fr.* Pineapple.

ANATRA (AH-nah-trah) *It.* Duck.

ANCHOIS (ahn-SHWAH) *Fr.* Anchovies.

ANGLAISE, À L' (ahn-GLAEZ) *Fr.* Boiled, of vegetables. Calf's liver, FOIE DE VEAU (fwah duh voh), English style is sautéed with bacon. Fish in this style, though, is generally coated with egg and bread crumbs and sautéed in butter; often served with Maître d'Hôtel butter, which see. But if it's SOLE ANGLAISE, it simply means English sole, Dover sole.

ANGUILLA, ANGUILLE (ahn-GWEEL-lah) *It.* (ahn-GEEY) *Fr.* Eel.

ANIMELLE (ah-nee-MAEL-lae) *It.* Sweetbread, which see.

ANITRA (AH-nee-trah) *It.* Duck.

ANNA (A-nah) *Fr.* A style of baking thinly sliced potatoes in butter in a casserole, producing a golden mound of potatoes.

ANTIPASTO (ahn-tee-PAH-stoh) *It.* Literally, before the meal, an appetizer.

ANTIPASTO MISTO (MEE-stoh) Mixed antipasto; generally a plate of raw vegetables and cold meats, eggs, fish, cheese.

ARAGOSTA (ah-rah-GOH-stah) *It.* Spiny or rock lobster.

ARANCIO (ah-RAHN-choh) *It.* Orange.

ARCHIDUC, À L' (ar-shih-DEWK) *Fr.* Prepared with paprika and cream.

AREGANATA Same as Arreganata, which see.

ARGENTEUIL (ar-zhahn-TUHY) *Fr.* Garnished with asparagus, especially white asparagus. Named for that region of France so famous for its asparagus.

ARINGA, ARINGHE (ah-REEN-gah, ah-REEN-gae) *It.* Herring.

ARISTA (ah-REE-stah) *It.* Roast loin of pork.

ARMAGNAC (ar-mah-NYAK) *Fr.* The brandy of the Armagnac region.

ARMORICAINE, À L' (ar-maw-rih-KAEN) *Fr.* Another spelling for Américaine, which see.

AROMATES, AUX (oh za-roh-MAT) *Fr.* Prepared with aromatic herbs and flavoring vegetables such as parsley, thyme, bay leaf, rosemary, tarragon, garlic, onion, shallots, chives, and celery.

ARRABBIATA (ahr-rahb-BYAH-tah) *It.* Literally, in a rage, which refers to the hot chili peppers used in the sauce (although, on one menu I've seen, the Pollo Arrabbiata was translated as "chicken in a white wine sauce," and I can't help but wonder if it might not also have described the unsuspecting diner as well). The sauce also contains olive oil, butter, and white wine.

ARREGANATA (ahr-rae-gah-NAH-tah) *It.* Prepared with oregano; frequently clams, VONGOLE (VOHN-goh-lae), sprinkled with chopped oregano, oil, and often bread crumbs, and baked in their shells.

ARROSTO, ARROSTITO (ahr-ROH-stoh, ahr-roh-STEE-toh) *It.* A roast; roasted, of meat.

ARROZ CON POLLO (ah-ROTH kawn POH-yoh) *Sp.* A dish of saffron rice with chicken, cooked with onion, sweet peppers, frequently also tomatoes, and often garnished with peas or asparagus tips, perhaps artichoke hearts; sometimes cooked with a little ham also.

ARRUGULA (ahr-ROO-goo-lah) *It.* An aromatic salad green with a somewhat nutlike flavor, called in English rocket or rockette.

ARTICHAUT (ar-tee-SHOH) *Fr.* Artichoke.

FOND D'ARTICHAUT (fawn) Artichoke bottom,

10

or heart.

ARUGULA (ah-ROO-goo-lah) *It.* Same as arrugula, which see.

ASPERGES (as-PAERZH) *Fr.* Asparagus.

ASPIC Jellied broth, used to glaze cold vegetables or meat, often in a molded shape. Chopped aspic is used as a garnish for Paté, etc.

ASSIETTE, L' (as-SYET) *Fr.* A plate, as in a cold plate or a platter of specialties.

AUBERGINE (oh-baer-ZHEEN) *Fr.* Eggplant.

AVEC (a-VEK) *Fr.* With.

AVGOLEMONO (ahv-goh-LE-moh-noh) *Gk.* The smooth soup of Greece and the Balkans, made with bouillon, usually chicken bouillon, egg, lemon juice, and rice.

AVOCADO PEAR This is simply an avocado.

BABAS AU RHUM (ba-BA zoh rawm) *Fr.* Little cakes made with flour, milk, eggs, yeast, and originally raisins and currants, though these are often omitted nowadays. The cakes are baked in special molds then soaked in rum and sugar syrup. Supposed to have been invented in the eighteenth century by King Stanislas I of Poland and named for Ali Baba, a character in one of his favorite books *(A Thousand and One Nights)*.

BAGNA CALDA (BAH-nyah KAH-dah) *It.* Same as Bagna Cauda, which see.

BAGNA CAUDA (BAH-nyah KAH-oo-dah) *It.* Literally, a hot bath. This is a do-it-yourself dish. The diners dip raw vegetables into a sauce of oil and butter flavored with garlic and anchovy, and, optionally (optional outside of Piedmont, at least), a slice of white truffle, and sometimes cream. The sauce is kept hot over a flame or heater and warms up as well as seasons the vegetables. In Piedmont

11

where this is a specialty, cardoons—of the thistle and artichoke family—are a favorite for dipping, but any variety of vegetables, within reason, may be used. Sometimes breadsticks are also dipped.

BAKED ALASKA This is a thick slice of ice cream on a slice of sponge cake, often sprinkled with liqueur, encased in meringue (whipped egg whites and sugar), and browned in the oven. It is often flamed. It is believed to have been invented by an American physicist, Benjamin Thompson, Count Rumford, in the late eighteenth or early nineteenth century. We don't know what he called his invention; the dessert is believed to have been christened "Baked Alaska" in the 1870s at Delmonico's Restaurant in New York City in honor of the purchase of the Alaska territory from Russia.

BALLOTINE, BALLOTTINE (bal-loh-TEEN) *Fr.* This "little bundle" is an elegant roll of boned meat, usually poultry, stuffed with ground meat, liver or liver paté, and flavored with herbs, spices, and seasoning vegetables such as onion and garlic, sometimes truffles, and brandy. It is braised or poached, and generally served hot, but sometimes cold.

BAR (bar) *Fr.* Sea bass.

BAR RAYÉ (rae-YAE) Striped bass.

BARQUETTE (bar-KET) *Fr.* A pastry shell in the shape of a little boat, which may hold sweet or savory fillings.

BASILICO (bah-ZEE-lee-koh) *It.* Basil.

BASQUAISE, À LA (bas-KAEZ) *Fr.* This generally describes dishes served with a garnish of potatoes cooked in butter, mushrooms (cèpes), and dices of the famous Bayonne ham of the Basque region.

BAVARIAN or BAVARIAN CREAM See Bavaroise.

BAVAROISE (ba-va-RWAHZ) *Fr.* A light custard made of eggs, sugar, and whipped cream and flavored with a wide variety of fruits and/or liqueurs (but not all at the same time, of course). This is often served in a molded form, in which case gelatin has been added to hold its shape.

BAY SCALLOPS The tiny scallops caught in bays, tenderer and more delicately flavored than the larger, deep sea scallops.

BAYONNE, JAMBON DE (zhahn-BAWn duh ba-yawn) *Fr.* The famous ham of Bayonne in France.

BÉARNAISE (be-ar-NAEZ) *Fr.* A rich sauce of beaten egg yolks, butter, and wine vinegar, flavored with shallots and tarragon, sometimes chervil.

BEEFSTEAK AND KIDNEY PUDDING *Br.* A classic English dish, and not exactly a pudding as we know pudding; it's more like a deep-dish meat pie, with suet crust traditionally, filled with a stew of beef chunks, sliced kidneys, onions, and sometimes mushrooms, simmered in red wine and/or broth.

BEIGNETS (be-NYE) *Fr.* These may be fritters, made with various types of food—fruit, vegetables, fish, etc.—dipped in batter and deep fried. Or they may be a sort of doughnut ball, made with a batter of flour, butter, sugar, water or milk, and eggs, deep fried, and sprinkled with confectioners' sugar.

BELLE HÉLÈNE (bel ae-LEN) *Fr.* Same as Hélène, which see.

BELLEVUE, EN (ahn bel-VEW) *Fr.* A decorative, and sometimes elaborate, way of serving cold poached lobster, HOMARD (aw-MAR), or perhaps salmon, SAUMON (soh-MAWn). It is spread with mayonnaise and aspic and garnished with hard-boiled eggs, tomatoes, etc. Poultry or meat may also be prepared in this style. They are coated with aspic and Chaud-froid Sauce, and decorated.

BENEDETTE (bae-nae-DAET-tae) *It.* A preparation for eggs, UOVA, (WAW-vah), see Benedict.

BENEDICT, EGGS Poached eggs on slices of ham on toasted English muffins, topped with Hollandaise Sauce, made with egg yolks, butter, lemon juice or vinegar, and a little pepper.

BERCY (baer-SEE) *Fr.* A sauce made from shallots cooked in butter, white wine, and fish broth with a squirt of lemon juice for seafood dishes or meat broth for meats, sprinkled with parsley.

BETTERAVE (bae-TRAV) *Fr.* Beets.

BEURRE (buhr) *Fr.* Butter.

BEURRE BLANC (blahn) Butter beaten with minced shallots which have been cooked in vinegar and perhaps white wine.

BEURRE NOIR (nwahr) Butter browned to a deep hazelnut color and flavored with a touch of vinegar or lemon juice, and a sprinkling of parsley; capers are sometimes also added.

BIANCO, IN (een BYAHN-koh) *It.* Boiled—of fish, rice.

BIFTECK (bihf-TEK) *Fr.* Beefsteak.

BIGARADE (bih-ga-RAD) *Fr.* An orange sauce for duck, CANARD (ka-NAR), named for the bitter oranges (Seville oranges) with which it's made. The sauce is made of duck broth and sometimes white wine, thickened with a little flour or cornstarch and flavored with strips of the orange rind, orange and lemon juice, a little sugar, and often laced with an orange-based liqueur such as Curaçao or Grand Marnier.

BILLI BI (BEEL-lee BEE) *Fr.* Mussel soup made with shallots and onions cooked in butter, white wine, and fish broth, seasoned with thyme, parlsey, bay leaf, and enriched with cream and egg yolk, and of course mussels; served hot or cold. This soup is said to be named for William Leeds, for whom it was created, at Maxim's restaurant in Paris.

BISMARCK HERRING Herring fillets pickled in vinegar with sliced onion, mustard seed, and black pepper.

BISQUE (bihsk) *Fr.* A thick soup made from shellfish pounded and sieved, fish broth, and often white wine, flavorings and spices, perhaps a dash of sherry or brandy (cognac); thickened with cream and sometimes egg yolk and garnished with pieces of the shellfish.

BISTECCA, BISTECCHE (bee-STAEK-kah, bee-STAEK-kae) *It.* Beefsteak.

BISTECCHINA (bee-staek-KEE-nah) *It.* Little beef-steak—minute steak.

BLANC, BLANCHE (blahn, blahnsh) *Fr.* White.

BLANQUETTE (blahn-KET) *Fr.* A stew of veal, DE VEAU (duh voh), or lamb, D'AGNEAU (da-NYOH), simmered in broth with mushrooms, white onions, and flavoring vegetables (chopped celery, carrot, etc.), aromatic herbs such as thyme, bay leaf, and parsley, and a touch of lemon juice; thickened with egg yolks, butter and flour, perhaps cream, and sprinkled with parsley.

BLEU, AU (oh bluh) *Fr.* A method of poaching trout, TRUITE (trweet), in water or bouillon containing vinegar, which turns the skin of the fish a steely blue; served with melted butter.

BLINIS (BLEE-neez) *Rs.* A Russian specialty—crêpes—traditionally of buckwheat, served with melted butter, caviar (sometimes smoked salmon, herring, or sardines), and sour cream.

BLUE POINTS Oysters, of the variety cultivated in special beds off Blue Point, Long Island.

BOCCONCINI (bohk-kohn-CHEE-nee) *It.* Little

15

mouthfuls, tidbits.

BOEUF (buhf) *Fr.* Beef.

BOLLITA (bohl-LEE-tah) *It.* Boiled.

BOLLITO MISTO (bohl-LEE-toh MEE-stoh) *It.* A variety of meats—beef, veal, chicken, tongue, ham—boiled together in a broth seasoned with onion, celery, carrots, bay leaf, and served with pork sausage (boiled separately). Often accompanied with SALSA VERDE (SAHL-sah VAER-dae), a tart green sauce of olive oil, lemon juice or vinegar, capers, shallots, garlic, and anchovy.

BOLOGNESE, ALLA (boh-loh-NYAE-zae) *It.* In the style of Bologna, "the gastronomic capital of Italy," where the cooking is rich. Pasta is doused with Ragù sauce, which see. For chicken, POLLO (POHL-loh), or veal cutlets, COSTOLETTE (koh-stoh-LAET-tae), as they are prepared in Bologna, the meat is breaded or floured, sautéed in butter, and topped with a slice of Prosciutto and Parmesan cheese (Mozzarella is sometimes substituted) and cooked in a little white wine or broth.

BOMBE (bawmb) *Fr.* This dessert gets its name from being formed into a ball, but it comes in various other shapes as well. It is a mold of ice cream or ices, whipped cream, and fruit, or a combination of ice cream flavors.

BONNE FEMME (bawn fam) *Fr.* Prepared in the style of the good (honest and unsophisticated) woman. When poultry or meat is served in this style, it is cooked with pearl onions, chopped bacon, and often tiny potatoes and mushrooms. POTAGE BONNE FEMME (poh-TAHZH) is a soup of sliced leeks cooked in butter and simmered in chicken or veal broth with sliced potatoes, sometimes thickened with purée of potatoes or cream, and sprinkled with chervil leaves. SOLE

16

BONNE FEMME is poached in a sauce of shallots, or onions, mushrooms, white wine, and parsley. The sauce is thickened with a paste of butter and flour and often seasoned with a few drops of lemon.

BORDELAISE (bohr-du-LAEZ) *Fr.* A red (Bordeaux) wine sauce seasoned with shallots or onions browned in butter, tomato, beef marrow, broth, parsley, and perhaps a little thyme and nutmeg and chopped mushrooms. À LA BORDELAISE usually means served with this sauce, but can also mean served with mushrooms (cèpes) or even accompanied with artichokes and potatoes.

BORSCHT (bawrsht) The national soup of Russia and Poland with a wide variation in recipes. Basically, it is beet soup, or beet and cabbage soup, sometimes with other vegetables; served hot or cold with sour cream. It may include meat.

BOUILLABAISSE (boo-ya-BES) *Fr.* The famous Mediterranean fish stew made from a variety of fishes, eel, and sometimes but not always lobster (in fact, some purists insist that to include lobster is to ruin the stew). The broth is made from fish broth flavored with saffron—which also gives it its orange color—leeks or onions, garlic, olive oil or butter, fennel, thyme, sometimes rosemary, tomatoes, bay leaf, dried orange peel, and parsley. Traditionally, it is served in two bowls—one for the fish, the other for the bouillon, which is poured over slices of bread in the bowl.

BOUILLI (boo-YEE) *Fr.* Boiled.

BOUILLON (boo-YAWɴ) *Fr.* Clear broth from meat, fish, or vegetables.

BOUQUETIÈRE (book-TYAER) *Fr.* In the style of the flower girl; namely, garnished with a variety of buttered vegetables, as surrounding a roast, each in its own little group or "bouquet."

17

BOURGEOISE (boor-ZHWAHZ) *Fr.* Cooked in hearty, family style—with onions, carrots and bacon, sometimes turnips and celery.

BOURGOGNE, DE (duh boor-GAW-nyu) *Fr.* Of Burgundy; see Bourguignonne.

BOURGUIGNONNE (boor-gee-NYAWN) *Fr.* A red (Burgundy) wine-based sauce flavored with shallots, thyme, bay leaf, parsley, and a touch of hot cayenne pepper, and thickened with a butter and flour paste; some chefs also include chopped mushrooms. BOEUF À LA BOURGUIGNONNE (buhf) Burgundian beef. Sometimes mistakenly used to mean beef stew, the dish is actually the other way around—stewed beef: braised beef chunks in a rich gravy made with red wine, white onions, sautéed mushrooms, chopped carrot, celery, sometimes a bit of tomato, bacon, or salt pork, and flavored with thyme, bay leaf, and perhaps a splash of brandy, the sauce thickened to a gravy consistency with a flour-butter paste. Boiled potatoes are a traditional accompaniment.

ESCARGOTS À LA BOURGUIGNONNE (es-kar-GOH) This is something else again; here, à la Bourguignonne means as they (the snails) are prepared in Burgundy. The poached snails are baked in their shells in a sauce of Burgundy butter (also called snail butter)—a paste of butter, shallots, and/or garlic, parsley, and often a dash of lemon juice, sometimes also sprinkled with bread crumbs. Should be served very hot.

BOVOLINI (boh-voh-LEE-nee) *It.* Snails.

BRACIOLA, BRACIOLETTE (brah-CHOH-lah, brah-choh-LAET-tae) *It.* Cutlet or steak.

BRANZINO (brahn-TSEE-noh) *It.* Bass.

BRASATO (brah-ZAH-toh) *It.* Braised.

BRASCIOLE (brah-SHOH-lae) *It.* Meat slices rolled

around a stuffing of ground meat, perhaps cheese, bread crumbs, parsley, and spices, browned in oil or butter, and simmered in broth or wine, or a particular sauce.

BREAD PUDDING, *Br.* A traditional pudding made with milk, eggs, sugar, and of course little chunks of buttered bread—supposed to be stale bread, to vary the texture (no doubt created by some thrifty and inventive cook to use up the day-old bread), seasoned with cinnamon or nutmeg and often dotted with raisins or currants.

BRESAOLA (bre-ZAH-oh-lah) *It.* Dried salt beef, a specialty of the Valtellina region of Lombardy.

BRETAGNE, À LA (bru-TA-nyu) *Fr.* See à la Bretonne.

BRETONNE, À LA (bru-TAWN) *Fr.* In the style of Brittany. Generally this means the dish will be accompanied with white kidney beans in a Sauce Bretonne. SAUCE BRETONNE (sohs) is made with butter, onions, carrots or mushrooms, celery, leeks in white wine, meat or fish broth, depending on the dish, and cream.

BRIOCHE (bree-AWSH) *Fr.* A light, puffed pastry made with flour, yeast, butter, eggs, perhaps also milk and sugar; often hollowed out and filled with meat or poultry in a cream or other sauce.
EN BRIOCHE (ahn) Baked wrapped in brioche dough.

BROCHET (braw-SHAE) *Fr.* Pike.

BROCHETTE, EN (ahn braw-SHET) *Fr.* Spitted on a long skewer and, usually, grilled or broiled.

BRODETTO (broh-DAET-toh) *It.* Generally, fish soup—of the same Greek origin as Bouillabaisse—although other soups may use the name, as it really only means "little broth."
BRODETTO DI PESCE (dee PAE-shae) Fish

soup made of a combination of fishes and shellfish—which fishes depends on where it is made and the fresh fish available that morning. Sometimes made with saffron, sometimes tomato—a lot is left to the discretion of the chef.

BRODO, IN (een BROH-doh) *It.* In broth.

PASTINA IN BRODO (pah-STEE-nah) Tiny little egg noodle rings or dots in, usually, chicken broth.

BRUSCHETTA (broo-SKAET-tah) *It.* Garlic toast.

BUDINO (boo-DEE-noh) *It.* Pudding is the usual meaning, but in BUDINO DI POLLO (dee POHL-loh) it's mousse of chicken.

BUE (BOO-ae) *It.* Beef.

BURRO, AL (BOOR roh) *It.* With butter. Pasta al Burro is not served with just butter on top, though, but with grated cheese as well.

CACCIATORE, ALLA (kahch-chah-TOH-rae) *It.* Hunter style. In America, this style of preparation, especially when done with chicken, POLLO (POHL-loh), tends to mean the meat has been sautéed in oil and cooked in a sauce of tomatoes, mushrooms, onions, green pepper, garlic, red or white wine, perhaps a little Marsala or Sherry, and spices such as bay leaf, basil, parsley. In Italy it may also indicate a simpler tomato sauce, but there is another cacciatore sauce, often used for lamb, ABBACCHIO (ahb-BAHK-kyoh), but sometimes for chicken also, especially in Italy. For this style the meat is sometimes floured before sautéeing. It is cooked in an anchovy sauce made with olive oil, garlic, perhaps onions, white wine, a little wine vinegar, broth, anchovies, and rosemary if for lamb, or oregano and sometimes black olives for chicken.

CAEN, À LA MODE DE (mawd duh KAɴ) *Fr.* A method of stewing TRIPES (treep) as they do in the Norman town of Caen. The tripe is cooked very slowly in cider traditionally, but sometimes white wine is used, with sliced carrots, onions, leeks and garlic, ox or calf's foot or perhaps a veal knuckle, and laced with Calvados (apple brandy).

CAESAR SALAD The famous salad named for its creator (no, not Julius!—Caesar Cardini in a restaurant in Tiajuana). It is prepared at your table from romaine lettuce tossed with olive oil (the bowl having first been rubbed with garlic), a coddled or raw egg, the juice of a lemon, anchovies, grated Parmesan, croutons of garlic toast, and a generous sprinkling of freshly ground black pepper.

CAFÉ (ka-FAE) *Fr.* You know this one.

CAFÉ AU LAIT (oh lae) Equal parts of coffee and hot milk poured together into a large-sized cup.

CAFÉ BRÛLOT (brew-LOH) Literally, firebrand coffee, the firebrand here being a lump of sugar flamed with brandy or rum. The coffee is spiced with cinnamon, cloves, allspice, orange, and lemon peel.

CAFÉ DIABLE (dee-ABL) Coffee flamed with brandy, the flames presumably representing the devil in the name.

CAFÉ FILTRE (feeltr) Strong black coffee, served in demi-tasse cups.

CAFFÈ (kahf-FAE) *It.* Coffee.

CAFFÈ ESPRESSO (ae-SPRAES-soh) Very strong black coffee, best from an espresso machine. Served in small cups, often (in America, at least) with a lemon peel to be twisted and dropped into the cup.

CAFFELATTE (kahf-fae-LAHT-tae) Black coffee and hot milk poured in equal portions into a large cup.

CAILLE (KAH-yu) *Fr.* Quail.

CALAMARI (kah-lah-MAH-ree) *It.* Cuttlefish, squid.

CALDE (KAHL-dae) *It.* Hot, warm.

CALIFORNIA SALAD From a state known for its fine fruit: chopped fruits (fresh in the better restaurants) in their own juice with cottage cheese.

CALVADOS, AU (oh kal-va-DOHS) *Fr.* Prepared with Norman brandy, which is made from cider rather than wine.

CANADIAN BACON Very lean cured pork, from the loin.

CANAPÉ (ka-na-PAE) *Fr.* Tiny open-faced appetizer sandwich.

CANARD (ka-NAR) *Fr.* Duck.

CANETON (kan-TAWɴ) *Fr.* Duckling.

CANNELLONI (kahn-nael-LOH-nee) *It.* "Big tubes" of rolled-up pasta squares filled with chopped meat and spices, baked in a tomato and/or cream sauce and sprinkled with grated Parmesan cheese.

CANNOLI (kahn-NOH-lee) *It.* A Sicilian specialty; these "pipes" of crispy pastry are filled with Ricotta cheese and cream and flavored with Marsala, or vanilla, or chocolate, sometimes candied fruit, and dusted with confectioners' sugar.

CAPE CODS Oysters from that hook of land off Massachusetts.

CAPONATA (kah-poh-NAH-tah) *It.* Cubes of eggplant cooked in olive oil with peppers, celery, onion, tomato, green olives, perhaps black olives, capers, and sometimes other vegetables, and seasoned with vinegar and a little sugar, and sometimes anchovies and pine nuts. Serve cold as an appetizer, or hot as a side dish.

CAPONATINA (kah-poh-nah-TEE-nah) *It.* A little Caponata, which see.

CAPPELLETTI (kahp-pael-LAET-tee) *It.* "Little hats" of pasta filled with minced chicken, meat, and/or cheese, and spices, depending on the sauce which will go over them, or the broth which they will go into if they are served IN BRODO (een BROH-doh).

CAPPERI (kahp-PAE-ree) *It.* Capers.

CAPPONE (kahp-POH-nae) *It.* Capon.

CAPPUCCINO (kahp-poo-CHEE-noh) *It.* A coffee specialty made in a cappuccino machine. Hot milk is forced into strong black coffee. The resulting drink is pale brown in color, the shade of a Capuchin monk's robe.

CÂPRES (kahpr) *Fr.* Capers.

CARBONARA, ALLA (kahr-boh-NAH-rah) *It.* A sauce for Spaghetti ("little strings") or Rigatoni (ribbed tubes of pasta), done in the style of the charcoal burners. For us it is done in a chafing dish, at tableside generally. A specialty of Rome, the sauce is made with diced unsmoked bacon, or Prosciutto (air-dried ham), in this country perhaps our bacon or ham, sautéed in butter and olive oil flavored with garlic. Raw eggs, or perhaps just the yolks, beaten with Parmesan and traditionally Pecorino cheese and white wine or broth—some chefs add cream—sometimes parsley, and plenty of freshly ground black pepper are mixed with the cooked pasta and the meat, and it is all tossed together to heat through.

CARBONADE (kar-baw-NAD) *Fr.* Braised meat cooked in broth with seasonings.

CARCIOFINI (kahr-choh-FEE-nee) *It.* Artichoke hearts, or bottoms.

CARCIOFO (kahr-CHOH-foh) *It.* Artichoke.

CARDINAL (kar-dih-NAL) *Fr.* A sauce for seafood; fish broth and bits of lobster or lobster coral, a

23

touch of hot cayenne pepper, and an optional truffle mixed into a white sauce of flour, butter, and milk or a cream sauce.

CARNE (KAHR-nae) *It.* Meat.

CARPACCIO (kahr-PAH-choh) *It.* Very thin slices of raw beef fillet or sirloin.

CARRÉ (kar-RAE) *Fr.* Rack, rib roast.

CARROZZA, MOZZARELLA IN (moh-tsah-RAEL-lah een kahr-ROH-tsah) *It.* Mozzarella cheese "in a carriage"—a Neapolitan specialty. A slice of Mozzarella sandwiched in between two slices of bread, which has been dipped in milk, sometimes rolled in crumbs, dipped into egg, and deep fried. It may be served with a buttery anchovy sauce seasoned with capers and parsley and a touch of lemon juice.

CARTE, À LA (kart) *Fr.* According to the menu card. Each dish is priced individually so that you may choose as few or as many courses as you wish.

CARTOCCIO, IN (een kahr-TOH-choh) *It.* Literally, in a paper bag—which is how the dish is served, and cooked—steamed with herbs and seasonings, such as onion, celery, garlic, parsley, in an oiled paper bag. When opened at the table the steam and aromas escape.

CASA, ALLA or DELLA (DAE-lah KAH-zah) *It.* In the style of the house.

CASALINGA, ALLA (kah-zah-LEEN-gah) *It.* Home-style, homemade.

CASINO, OYSTERS or CLAMS Either of these shellfish in the half-shell sprinkled with chopped green pepper, onion or shallots, chives, sometimes pimento, and parsley, a squirt of lemon juice, and pieces of bacon, then baked or broiled.

CASSATA (kahs-SAH-tah) *It.* A Sicilian specialty. A dessert of sponge cake filled with sweetened Ricotta cheese flavored with liqueur and dotted with bits of chocolate, candied fruits and nuts, and sometimes ice cream. Frosting is sometimes spread on top, but confectioners' sugar may be dusted on instead.

CASSATA GELATA (kahs-SAH-tah jae-LAH-tah) *It.* A molded frozen dessert made of ice cream or frozen custard filled with whipped cream studded with candied fruit and sugared almonds, perhaps flavored with liqueur, and surrounded by a ring of sherbert.

CASSINO, CLAMS or OYSTERS See Casino

CASSOULET or CASSOULET TOULOUSAIN (kas-soo-LAE too-loo-ZAn) *Fr.* A casserole of white beans and meat—pork, ham, sausage, lamb, and goose or duck (not necessarily every kind, but there must be a good variety). The broth is seasoned with onion, garlic, and aromatic herbs such as clove, thyme, bay leaf, allspice, parsley.

CASSOLETTE (kas-saw-LET) *Fr.* A small, individual casserole containing hot or cold hors d'oeuvres in a sauce.

CASTAGNE (kah-STAH-nyae) *It.* Chestnuts.

CATALANE, À LA (ka-ta-LAN) *Fr.* Generally dishes made in the style of Catalonia will be cooked in olive oil with lots of garlic. It may also mean, though, that the dish is accompanied with diced eggplant and rice pilaf in tomato sauce.

CAVIALE (kah-VYAH-lae) *It.* Caviar.

CAVIAR True caviar is the eggs, or roe, of the sturgeon. The, black, Sevruga caviar is the smallest-grained caviar; Beluga (black or gray) has the largest eggs. Osetrova is in the middle. Malossol means low in salt. Caviar should be served ice cold. The eggs of other fish, such as the lump fish (dyed black to resemble true caviar), are also called caviar, but qualified by the name of the fish—

"lumpfish caviar." "Caviar," alone means sturgeon roe.

RED CAVIAR Not true caviar; this is the roe of the salmon.

CEDRO (CHAE-droh) *It.* Citron, lime.

CELESTINA, CÉLESTINE (chae-lae-STEE-nah) *It.* (sae-les-TEEN) *Fr.* A soup of beef or chicken consommé, flavored with a touch of chervil and parsley, in which crêpes cut into thin strips are floated.

CÈPES (sep) *Fr.* The wild, brown, Boletus mushroom.

CERISES (su-REEZ) *Fr.* Cherries.

CERVELLA, CERVELLES (chaer-VAEL-lah) *It.* (ser-VEL) *Fr.* Brains.

CERVO (CHAER-voh) *It.* Venison.

CHABLIS, AU (oh sha-BLEE) *Fr.* Prepared in white wine (Chablis); usually clams, which are chopped with garlic, shallots, parsley and chervil, mixed with a little butter, sprinkled with lemon juice and Chablis, and broiled in their half-shells.

CHAMPIGNONS (shan-pih-NYAWN) *Fr.* Mushrooms, especially the white button mushrooms.

CHANTERELLES, AUX (oh shahn-TREL) *Fr.* Prepared with a variety of wild, yellow, mushroom,

CHANTILLY (shahn-TEE-YEE) *Fr.* Unsweetened whipped cream flavored with vanilla.

CHAPON (sha-PAWN) *Fr.* Capon.

CHARLOTTE RUSSE (shar-LAWT ROOS) *Fr.* A molded dessert, created by the famous chef Carême. It is a light custard made with eggs, sugar, and whipped cream, vanilla or other flavor, ringed with slices of sponge cake or lady fingers. It may be topped with whipped cream, perhaps fruit, or with more of the sponge cake.

CHASSEUR (sha-SEWR) *Fr.* Hunter's sauce, made

with mushrooms sautéed in butter with shallots, white wine, and tomato—more or less of it depending on the chef—and sprinkled with parsley.

CHATEAUBRIAND, CHATEAUBRIANT (shah-toh-bree-AHN) *Fr.* A thick cut of steak from the tenderloin, or sometimes porterhouse. This particular cut is said to have been the invention of Montmireil, chef to Vicomte Châteaubriand.

CHAUD (shoh) *Fr.* Hot, warm.

CHAUD-FROID (shoh-FRWAH) *Fr.* Literally, hot-cold. This describes a dish which has been cooked, chilled, and is served cold under a coating of Chaud-froid Sauce. This sauce is made with the broth from the meat (or fish, or poultry) it will cover, plus cream and egg yolks, especially for poultry and fish, and unflavored gelatin. On meats, the cream may be omitted and a meaty, wine-based sauce, plus Sherry or Port, substituted. For duck, the sauce is somewhere in between the two—with cream and brown sauce plus liqueur. Bits of vegetables cut into decorative shapes are often incorporated into the sauce, which is itself often glazed with aspic.

CHEF SALAD A salad which makes a filling lunch all by itself. It is made up of fresh greens—Boston lettuce, romaine, etc.—topped with strips of chicken, turkey, ham, perhaps tongue, "Swiss" cheese, slices of boiled egg, and tomato quarters. Sometimes green peppers, celery, carrots, and/or radish are also included. The chef may even choose to toss in another vegetable or two. Topped with the salad dressing of your choice.

CHEMISE, EN (ahn shu-MEEZ) *Fr.* Literally, in a shirt. In this case, the shirt is usually a crêpe, or a wrapper of puff pastry.

CHERRYSTONES Hard-shelled clams, quahogs, a

little larger than the little necks, usually served raw on the half-shell.

CHEVAL, À (shu-VAL) *Fr.* Literally, on horseback. In restaurants we generally see three things on horseback:

BIFTECK À CHEVAL (beef-TEK) A steak topped with a fried egg or two. Not to be confused with steak *de* cheval, which is horsemeat.

HAMBURGER À CHEVAL A hamburger topped with a fried egg.

HUÎTRES À CHEVAL (hweetr za) Oysters wrapped in bacon, sprinkled with chopped parlsey, and broiled; served on pieces of fried bread or toast.

CHEVREUIL (shu-VREWY) *Fr.* Venison, roe-deer.

CHOIX, AU (oh shwah) *Fr.* Of choice, yours.

CHORON (shoh-ROHN) *Fr.* A sauce made with egg yolks, butter, and tomato purée flavored with shallots and tarragon, perhaps chervil and a touch of wine vinegar.

CHOU (shoo) *Fr.* Cabbage.

CHOU (VERT) FARCI (vaer far-SEE) Stuffed green cabbage leaves. The stuffing varies, of course, but ground meat—beef, pork, or veal—spices, and tomato sauce or meat gravy are likely to be in the dish.

CHOUCROUTE (shoo-KROOT) *Fr.* Sauerkraut. Alsatian sauerkraut is seasoned with juniper berries (the ones that give gin its distinctive flavor.)

CHOUCROUTE GARNIE or ALSACIENNE (gar-NEE, al-za-SYEN) Sauerkraut braised in bacon or goose fat and cooked in white wine or broth with sliced carrots and onions, bacon or salt pork, ham and sausages, and seasoned with bay leaf, clove, and parsley. Served surrounded with the sausages, sliced ham, pork, perhaps smoked pork or

28

goose—the variety is flexible—and garnished with boiled potatoes.

CHOUCROUTE STRASBOURGEOISE (stras-boor-ZHWAHZ) Describing this dish as in the style of the Alsatian city of Strasbourg usually means that it will be garnished with, along with the usual variety of meats, Strasbourg sausages made from pork and beef and perhaps veal, and seasoned with garlic and lightly smoked. Otherwise, it's pretty much the same as Choucroute Garnie or Alsacienne.

CHUTNEY A sweet-sour relish of chopped vegetables, fruits, and spices; of East Indian origin.

CILIEGIE (chee-LYAE-jae) *It.* Cherries.

CINGALAISE (san-ga-LAEZ) *Fr.* Dishes described as in the style of Ceylon are seasoned with curry.

CIOCCOLATA (chohk-koh-LAH-tah) *It.* Chocolate.

CIOPPINO (chohp-PEE-noh) A California stew of mixed seafood, reputedly based on a stew made by the Italian fishermen of old San Francisco. And it sounds like a pretty good theory; they do make a stew of mixed seafood in Liguria which they call in the local dialect "ciuppin." Cioppino is made from chopped onion, garlic, green pepper, scallions, and tomato cooked in olive oil, and white wine seasoned with basil, and perhaps bay leaf, and a variety of fish and shellfish. These may include chunks of fresh fish, shrimp, crab, and clams or oysters in their shells—the variety depending on the morning's catch, in the Ciuppin tradition. This is a rich stew, heavy on the seafood and light on the liquid—or should be.

CIPOLLE (chee-POHL-lae) *It.* Onions.

CITRON (sih-TRAWN) *Fr.* A citrus fruit in the lemon family. Generally only the thick skin is used, candied, in desserts.

CLAMART, À LA (kla-MAR) *Fr.* Green peas figure in a dish done in this style—classically, in artichoke bottoms as a garnish, but may also be in a stuffing or other garnish.

CLUB SANDWICH A double-decker sandwich made with three slices of toast. The two fillings are white meat chicken on lettuce with mayonnaise, and sliced tomatoes and fried bacon with mayonnaise (b,l,t). Ham, cheese, or other fillings are sometimes also used. The sandwich is served cut into wedges, the layers held together on a toothpick, and often garnished with green olives or pickle slices.

COBBLER A deep-dish fruit pie with a thick pastry crust on the top only, over the chopped fruit—cherries, peaches, etc.—in syrup.

COCHON DE LAIT (koh-SHAWn duh LAE) *Fr.* Suckling pig(let).

COCKLES You may never run across this item on the menu, except perhaps in an English seafood restaurant, but haven't you always wondered what the heck it is "alive, alive-o." No? Well, for those of you who have, they're a variety of shellfish related to the oyster.

COCKTAIL, SEAFOOD A preparation of boiled, chilled shellfish—shrimp, crabmeat, lobster meat—arranged on lettuce or perhaps crushed ice and served with a tangy tomato sauce made with ketchup, Worcestershire sauce, lemon juice, perhaps dry mustard, and chives, garlic and onion, and sometimes also chili sauce, and sparked with horseradish or Tabasco sauce. In Europe, they usually serve a different kind of cocktail sauce, a mayonnaise-based sauce sometimes with a touch of tomato, on seafood cocktail.

COCOTTE, EN (ahn kaw-KAWT) *Fr.* Cooked in a casserole and/or served in an individual casserole dish.

CODA (KOH-dah) *It.* Tail.

CODA DI BUE (dee BOO-ae) Oxtail.

CODFISH CAKES, NEW ENGLAND Disks of flaked codfish mixed with mashed potato and egg, fried or deep-fried.

COEUR (kuhr) *Fr.* Heart.

COEUR DE LA CRÈME or À LA CRÈME (duh la krem) A dessert of cream cheese whipped with heavy cream and egg whites and sprinkled with sugar, sometimes formed into a heart shape, and surrounded with strawberries.

COLBERT (kohl-BAER) *Fr.* A method of preparing fish, which are coated with egg and bread crumbs and fried, and served with SAUCE COLBERT (sohs) made with butter, tarragon or parsley, a dash of lemon juice, and sometimes a little Madeira.

COMPOTE A mixture of fruits cooked in sugar syrup; sometimes brandy or other liquor is added to the sauce.

CON (kohn) *It.* With.

CONCHIGLIE (kohn-KHEE-lyae) *It.* Conch; or, if pasta—shells.

CONCOMBRES (kawn-KAWnBR) *Fr.* Cucumbers.

CONFITTURA, CONFITURES (kohn-feet-TOO-rah) *It.* (kawn-fee-TEWR) *Fr.* Fruit preserves, jam.

CONIGLIO (koh-NEE-lyoh) *It.* Rabbit.

CONSOMMÉ (kawn-saw-MAE) *Fr.* Clear meat or chicken broth flavored with herbs and seasonings.

CONSOMMÉ DOUBLE (doobl) Double-strength consommé, fortified with Sherry or Maderia, and sometimes a dash of lemon is added.

CONTADINA (kohn-tah-DEE-nah) *It.* Peasant style;

31

prepared in a sauce of tomatoes, mushrooms, sweet peppers, and sometimes Sherry (for well-to-do peasants).

COPERTO (koh-PAER-toh) *It.* Cover charge, or a charge for the bread on the table (whether you eat it or not).

COPPA (KOHP-pah) *It.* Cup, as in fruit cup, COPPA DI FRUTTA (dee FROOT-tah); also, a cup of ice cream with a topping. But COPPA DI TESTA (TAE-stah), sometimes also referred to simply as Coppa, is headcheese, quite a different thing altogether.

COQ AU VIN (kohk oh van) *Fr.* Chicken in wine, specifically chicken sautéed in oil and stewed in a red wine gravy, sometimes thickened with a little ground-up chicken liver, and seasoned with garlic, thyme, bay leaf, blazed brandy, and bacon, and cooked with carrot, whole white onions, and sliced sautéed mushrooms. I was once told by a Frenchman how Coq au Vin was first made. It was an accident. The castle cook put the pieces of chicken into the pot with the seasoning vegetables and herbs, poured in a little broth, and left it to simmer over the fire. Along came a clumsy (tipsy?) servant lad carrying a jug of red wine. Sure enough, he stumbled just as he was leaning over to peek into the pot to see what smelled so good. In splashed the wine. And out dashed the culprit, fearing the beating he'd get from the cook. By the time the cook discovered the damage, it was too late. The king was stopping that night for dinner, and the chicken would have to be served. The king loved the dish, pronouncing it an inspired creation. And chefs have been making it on purpose ever since.

COQUILLAGES (kaw-kee-AHZH) *Fr.* Shellfish.

COQUILLE, EN (ahn kaw-KEEY) *Fr.* In their shells, on the half-shell.

COQUILLES DE FRUITS DE MER (kaw-KEEY duh FRWEET duh MAER) *Fr.* Mixed seafood ("fruits of the sea") prepared in the same way as Coquille Saint-Jacques, which see.

COQUILLES SAINT-JACQUES (kaw-KEEY san zhahk) *Fr.* Actually, this is simply the French term for scallops, but when listed on the menu without a qualification it stands for COQUILLES SAINT-JACQUES À LA PARISIENNE (pa-ree-ZYEN). The scallops, as they are prepared in Paris, are poached in white wine with herbs, shallots, and sautéed mushrooms. The sauce is enriched with butter and flour, cream and egg yolks, poured over the scallops in their shells, squirted with lemon juice, sprinkled with grated cheese, and browned under a flame.

CORDON BLEU (kawr-DAWN bluh) *Sw.* Literally, blue ribbon. A Swiss style of preparing veal cutlets, KALBSCHNITZEL (KAHLP-shniht-tsel), usually, but breast of chicken is often prepared in the same way. The meat is stuffed with a slice of Emmenthal (Swiss) cheese and a slice of ham, breaded and sautéed.

COSTA, COSTATA (KOH-stah, koh-STAH-tah) *It.* Chop, ribsteak.

COSTOLETTA (koh-stoh-LAET-tah) *It.* Cutlet, chop.

CÔTE (koht) *Fr.* Chop, ribsteak.

CÔTELETTE, (koh-TLET) *Fr.* COTOLETTA, (koh-toh-LAET-tah) *It.* Chop, cutlet.

COTTO (KOHT-toh) *It.* Cooked.

COULIBIAC See Kulibiaka.

COUPE (koop) *Fr.* Cup; usually an ice cream dessert topped with a sauce and perhaps whipped cream.
COUPE DE FRUITS (duh frwee) Fruit salad.
COUPE AUX MARRONS (aw mar-RAWN) Vanilla ice cream topped with chestnuts in syrup.

COUPE GLACÉE (gla-SAE) This is the French version of what we call a sundae.

COUVERT (koo-VAER) *Fr.* Cover charge.

COZZE (KOH-tsae) *It.* Mussels.

CRÉCY, À LA (krae-SEE) *Fr.* Made with, or garnished with carrots, especially glazed carrots. Named after the little French town of Crécy, famous for its carrots.

CREMA (KRAE-mah) *It.* Custard.

CREMA ALLA CARAMELLA or CARAMEL-LATA (kah-rah-MAEL-lah, kah-rah-mael-LAH-tah) Egg custard unmolded onto a plate upside down, putting the caramel (burnt sugar) syrup from the bottom of the cup on top.

CRÈME (krem) *Fr.* Cream, cream soup, or dessert creams or custards.

CRÈME CARAMEL (ka-ra-MEL) Egg custard unmolded onto a plate bottom side up with the caramel (burnt sugar) now on the top; sometimes called CRÈME RENVERSÉE AU CARAMEL (rahn-ver-SAE oh)—upside down caramel custard.

CRÉOLE (krae-AWL) *Fr.* A tomato sauce seasoned with onions or shallots, sometimes green peppers, pimientos, garlic, hot cayenne pepper, and wine.

CRÊPES (krep) *Fr.* The delicately thin, light French version of a pancake, made with sweet fillings and/ or sauces for desserts, but also stuffed with seafood, chicken, etc., for appetizer or entrées.

CRÊPE SUZETTE (sew-ZET) A flaming dessert prepared at your table. The crêpes are heated in a sauce of caramelized sugar and butter, the juice of an orange and a lemon, and flamed with Cognac and Grand Marnier, or similar liqueurs, and usually garnished with thin strips of orange and/or lemon peel.

CRESSON (kre-SAWn) *Fr.* Watercress.

CREVETTES (kru-VET) *Fr.* Shrimp.

CREVETTES ROSES (rohz) A variety of shrimp with a rosy pink color on the outside.

CROCCHETTE (krohk-KAET-tae) *It.* Same as Croquettes, which see.

CROISSANTS (krwah-SAHN) *Fr.* Flaky, delicate, buttery crescent-shaped pastry rolls.

CROQUE MONSIEUR (krawk mu-SYUH) *Fr.* Hot ham and Gruyère cheese sandwich, sometimes dipped in egg or egg and crumbs, baked or sautéed in butter, and perhaps browned with a crust of grated cheese; it may even be topped with a cheese sauce.

CROQUETTES (kraw-KET) *Fr.* Minced meat, poultry, fish, or vegetables formed into a shape—cone, cylinder, or whatever—bound together with a cream or milk and egg sauce, coated with egg and bread crumbs, and fried or deep fried.

CROSTATA (kroh-STAH-tah) *It.* Pie, tart.

CROSTINI (kroh-STEE-nee) *It.* Toasts. This includes the toast floated in soups and toasts topped with tasty spreads or bits of goodies, like canapés.

CROSTINI ALLA PROVATURA (proh-vah-TOO-rah) A specialty of Rome, named for the type of cheese originally used, Provatura. Mozzarella is much more common nowadays. These are pieces of toast and pieces of cheese threaded alternately on skewers (or placed together without the skewers), baked in the oven, then spread with anchovy butter.

CROUSTADE (kroos-TAD) *Fr.* Pastry shell, or hollowed-out roll or crustless loaf of bread, toasted or deep fried, filled with cooked fish, meat, or poultry in a sauce.

CROÛTE (kroot) *Fr.* A crust. This may be a crust of bread (toast) with a savory topping or filling,

35

Canapés, for example, or the toast floated in your onion soup.

EN CROÛTE (ahn) In a crust. In this case, a pastry crust as with roast meat wrapped in a pastry crust and baked.

CRUDO (KROO-doh) *It.* Raw, uncooked.

BROCCOLI A CRUDO (BRAWK-koh-lee) In this case, though, the broccoli is cooked—sautéed in oil with garlic and steamed in white wine.

CRUDITÉS (krew-dee-TAE) *Fr.* Raw vegetables, such as green onion, carrots, celery, olives, cauliflower, etc.

CRUSTACÉS (krew-sta-SAE) *Fr.* Crustaceans—crab, crayfish, lobster, shrimp.

CUISSES (kwees) *Fr.* Legs—of chicken, frogs.

CUISSEAU (kwee-SOH) *Fr.* Leg (of veal).

CUISSOT (kwee-SOH) *Fr.* Haunch (of venison).

CUIT (kwee) *Fr.* Cooked.

CUMBERLAND SAUCE, *Br.* A traditional English sauce for game made with red currant jelly, Port, chopped glazed cherries, orange and lemon rind, and the juice of those two, a touch of vinegar, and a sprinkle of hot cayenne pepper.

CURAÇAO (kewr-ah-SOW) An orange-based liqueur.

DARNE (darn) *Fr.* A fish steak, usually a slice on the bone.

DAUBE (dohb) *Fr.* A stew of braised meat, usually beef, cooked in meat broth or red wine with carrots and onions or shallots, perhaps garlic and a little salt pork, and flavoring herbs such as parsley, bay leaf, and thyme. The cover of the pot is sealed on with a flour-water paste, and the stew is simmered slowly.

DAUPHINOISE, À LA (doh-fan-WAHZ) *Fr.* Prepared with a garnish of scalloped potatoes done in the style of the Dauphiné, POMME DE TERRE DAUPHINOISE (pawm duh taer) or GRATIN DAUPHINOIS (gra-TAn doh-fan-WAH). Potatoes in this style are thinly sliced and baked in butter and cream or milk (beaten eggs may also be added) and often topped with grated cheese, especially when listed as Gratin Dauphinois.

DEMI (du-MEE) *Fr.* Half.

DEMI-DEUIL (du-mee DUHY) *Fr.* Literally, in half-mourning. A preparation for poultry in which slices of truffles are slipped under the skin, the bird is poached, then served with a garnish of sweetbreads and a cream sauce made with the broth, butter and flour, cream and egg yolks.

DEMI-TASSE (du-mee-TAS) *Fr.* A little cup of strong black coffee.

DENTE, AL (DAEN-tae) *It.* Literally, to the tooth; slightly resistant to the tooth, that is. The way pasta should be cooked: until it is springy firm, slightly chewy, not soft and mushy.

DÉSOSSÉ (dae-zaw-SAE) *Fr.* Boned, boneless.

DEVILED Cooked, or served, with a pungent sauce often containing mustard, pepper, or hot (as the devil) pepper. Deviled dishes are frequently breaded.

DIANE, STEAK As created by Nino, chef at the Drake Hotel in New York City, this is a thin steak sautéed in butter with shallots at your table. It is sometimes flamed with Cognac; chives may take the place of the original shallots, and Sherry is occasionally added to the sauce.

DIAVOLA, ALLA (DYAH-voh-lah) *It.* "As the devil." Here, hot as the devil; often, grilled chicken, POLLO (POH-loh), sprinkled with hot pepper, or with plenty of black pepper and/or ginger.

37

DIEPPOISE, À LA (dyep-PWAHZ) *Fr.* A style of preparing saltwater fish named for the French seaport. The fish is cooked in a white wine sauce with mussels and shrimp, and occasionally also mushrooms.

DIJONNAISE (dee-zhoh-NAEZ) *Fr.* Any dish described thus will be prepared with a mustard sauce, more correctly, a sauce made with the pungent mustard of Dijon, and eggs, oil, and lemon juice.

DINDE, DINDONNEAU (dand, dan-daw-NOH) *Fr.* Turkey hen, young turkey, respectively. Originally spelled "d'Inde"—of India—referring presumably to the West Indies, this being a New World bird.

DOLCE, DOLCI (DOHL-chae, DOHL-chee) *It.* Sweet; sweets (dessert).

DOLMAS (DOHL-mahs) *Trk.* Literally, stuffed; usually vine leaves (but might even refer to stuffed eggplant or other vegetable). The vine leaves are stuffed with a mixture such as rice, ground lamb, chopped onion, olive oil, parsley, dill, and lemon juice, served as an entrée. As an appetizer, Dolmas will usually be stuffed with rice in oil with perhaps lemon juice and spices such as nutmeg and pepper.

DORIA (DAW-ryah) *Fr.* A preparation for fish, especially salmon. SAUMON (soh-MAWN), which is sautéed in butter with chunks of cucumber, and perhaps garlic, and sprinkled with parsley.

DOVER SOLE   English (Channel) sole.

DU BARRY (dew bar-REE) *Fr.* A dish bearing the name of Louis XV's favorite will be garnished with cauliflower buds; classically, topped with a cream sauce and grated cheese.
CRÈME DU BARRY (krem) Cream of cauliflower soup.

DUCHESSE, À LA (dew-SHES) *Fr.* Garnished with potatoes mashed with cream, butter, and egg, seasoned with a touch of nutmeg, and browned in the oven.

DUGLÈRE (dew-GLER) *Fr.* A sauce for seafood made with butter, onion, garlic, white wine, and/or fish broth, chopped tomatoes, and thickened with egg and a flour-butter paste, seasoned with thyme, bay leaf, and parsley.

DUXELLES (dewk-SEL) *Fr.* Chopped mushrooms sautéed in butter with minced shallots and onions, used as a stuffing. Or, as a sauce, cooked with white wine, a touch of tomato, and sprinkled with parsley.

E (ae) *It.* And.

ÉCHALOTE (e-sha-LAWT) *Fr.* Shallot.

ÉCOSSE, SAUMON D' (soh-MAWn dae-KAWS) *Fr.* Scotch salmon; smoked salmon more delicate in flavor, lighter in color, and without the saltiness of Nova Scotia salmon.

ÉCREVISSES (ae-kru-VEES) *Fr.* Freshwater crayfish.

ÉMINCÉ (ae-man-SAE) *Fr.* Thin slices (of meat) cooked or heated up in any one of a number of different sauces.

ENTRECÔTE (ahn-tru-KOHT) *Fr.* A steak cut from the ribs, or sometimes the sirloin.

ENTREMETS (ahn-tru-MAE) *Fr.* Literally, between dishes; these used to be side dishes served with the second course. Nowadays the term is used to mean the dessert course served after the cheese.

ÉPAULE (ae-POHL) *Fr.* Shoulder.

ÉPINARDS (ae-pee-NAR) *Fr.* Spinach.

ESCALOPE (es-ka-LAWP) *Fr.* A boneless slice of meat flattened with a cutlet bat.

ESCARGOTS (es-kar-GOH) *Fr.* Snails.

ESPADON (es-pa-DAWn) *Fr.* Swordfish.

ESPAGNOLE, À L' (aes-pa-NYAWL) *Fr.* Spanish

style: cooked in oil with chopped tomatoes, onions, garlic, sweet peppers, and paprika.

ESPRESSO (ae-SPRAES-soh) *It.* Very strong black coffee, sometimes from an espresso machine, served in small cups. In America a lemon peel is often served with the coffee, to be twisted and dropped into the cup.

ESTOUFADE, ESTOUFFADE (es-too-FAD) *Fr.* Simply stated, beef stew. This is chunks of beef stewed in red wine with onions, garlic, often mushrooms, carrots, celery, and herbs such as bay leaf, parsley, and thyme.

ESTRAGON (es-tra-GAWn) *Fr.* Tarragon.

ESTURGEON (es-tewr-ZHAWn) *Fr.* Sturgeon.

ET (ae) *Fr.* And.

FAÇON, À LA (fa-SAWn) *Fr.* In the fashion, in the style.

FAGIANO (fah-JAH-noh) *It.* Pheasant.

FAGIOLI (fah-JOH-lee) *It.* White kidney beans.

PASTA E FAGIOLI (PAH-stah ae) You might know this as "pasta fazool." A soup of white beans and broken spaghetti thickened with a purée of the same beans. It may be seasoned with sautéed onions and a bit of tomato paste and cooked in beef broth, or made with chopped onion, garlic, carrot, and celery cooked in oil, salt pork and/or ham, and sprinkled with grated Parmesan cheese.

FAGIOLINI (fah-joh-LEE-nee) *It.* French beans, string beans.

FAISAN (fu-ZAn) *Fr.* Pheasant.

FARCI (far-SEE) *Fr.* Stuffed.

FAVE (FAH-vae) *It.* Broad beans, fava beans.

FEGATO (FAE-gah-toh) *It.* Liver.

FEGATINI (fae-gah-TEE-nee) *It.* "Little livers," chicken livers.

FENOUIL (fu-NOOY) *Fr.* Fennel.

FERMIÈRE, À LA (faer-MYAER) *Fr.* Farmer's style: cooked with sliced carrots, turnips, celery, and onions sautéed in butter.

FETTUCCINE (faet-too-CHEE-nae) *It.* Literally, little ribbons. The ribbon noodles of Rome, ¼ to ½ inch wide, depending on who's doing the slicing. The counterpart to Bologna's Tagliatelle.

FEUILLETAGE, DE (duh fuhy-TAZH) *Fr.* In "leaves" of flaky pastry dough.

FEUILLETÉE, EN (ahn fuhy-TAE) *Fr.* Same as de Feuilletage, which see.

FÈVES (fev) *Fr.* Shell beans, broad beans—fava beans.

FIAMMA, ALLA (FYAHM-mah) *It.* Flamed, with brandy or other liquor.

FICHI (FEE-kee) *It.* Figs, fresh or dried depending on the dish.

FIGUES, AUX (oh feeg) *Fr.* With figs.

FILETTO (fee-LAET-toh) *It.* Fillet; sometimes filet steak.

FINANCIÈRE (fih-nahn-SYAER) *Fr.* A rich sauce of Madeira, meat broth, mushrooms, truffles, sometimes chicken livers and olives.

FINE CHAMPAGNE, AU (oh feen shan-PAN-yu) *Fr.* Prepared with—nope, not the bubbly stuff—fine champagne brandy (Cognac).

FINES HERBES, AUX (oh feen zaerb) *Fr.* Made with a combination of chopped parsley, chervil, tarragon, and sometimes chives; or chopped parsley alone, as in Omelette aux Fines Herbes.

FINNAN HADDIE, *Sc.* Golden-colored smoked haddock of the Scottish town of Findon.

FINOCCHIO (fee-NOHK-kyoh) *It.* Fennel, either the seeds or the vegetable itself.

FIORENTINA, ALLA (fyoh-raen-TEE-nah) *It.* In

the style of Florence (Firenza), where food is prepared simply, with high-quality ingredients. Alla Fiorentina sometimes describes a dish prepared with spinach, not that Florence uses a lot of spinach in its cooking. But the Medicis of Florence apparently enjoyed this vegetable before most other Italians when it was first imported into Europe from the Middle East. So, perhaps, spinach became identified with Florence at that time.

ARISTA FIORENTINA (ah-REE-stah) Roast loin of pork as they make it in Florence is seasoned with rosemary.

BISTECCA ALLA FIORENTINA (bee-STAEK-kah) A T-bone or porterhouse steak prepared in the style of Florence (Firenza) is seasoned with olive oil, salt and pepper, and grilled, over a charcoal fire, traditionally; often served garnished with lemon wedges.

FLAGEOLETS (fla-zhaw-LAE) *Fr.* Small, green, navy-type beans, traditionally served with roast lamb.

FLAMANDE, À LA (fla-MAND) *Bl.* In the Flemish (Belgian) style; a method of preparing braised beef (Vlaamse Karbonaden). Beef and sliced onions are sautéed, then stewed in dark beer seasoned with parsley, thyme, bay leaf, and perhaps garlic, a dash of wine vinegar, and a spoon of sugar. In the true Flemish style the sauce is thickened with a slice of dark bread spread with mustard which dissolves in the cooking.

FLAMBÉ (flahn-BAE) *Fr.* Flamed with brandy or other liquor.

FLAN (flahn) *Sp.* In Spanish restaurants this is egg custard with burnt sugar topping, a caramel custard. In French, FLAN (flahn) is the same as Tarte—a pastry crust filled with fruit, custard, or other filling.

FLOATING ISLANDS A dessert of "islands" of meringue (egg whites whipped with sugar) poached in sweetened milk and served, cold, in a dish of custard made with milk, egg yolks, and sugar, flavored with vanilla. Sometimes caramel syrup is drizzled over the top.

FLORENTINE, À LA (flaw-rahn-TEEN) *Fr.* A style of cooking named for the Italian city of Florence. The meat, fish, poultry, or eggs are served on a bed of chopped spinach, and often topped with a sauce made up of butter and flour, milk, broth, heavy cream, sometimes egg yolk, and a sprinkle of nutmeg, and topped with grated cheese browned in the oven.

FOIE (fwah) *Fr.* Liver.

FOIE GRAS (fwah grah) *Fr.* Literally, fat liver, or more precisely, fattened liver. The liver, usually of geese, D'OIE (dwah), but may be of ducks, DE CANARD (duh ka-NAR), which has been enlarged by force-feeding of the birds. A gastronomic delicacy known since Roman times.

PÂTÉ DE FOIE GRAS (pah-TAE duh) is a pâté of this rich, specially fattened liver. Fresh foie gras is processed and packed, usually, into loaf forms but also into crocks. The canned foie gras has been partially cooked. Foie Gras may be truffled, TRUFFÉ (TREW-FAE), or not. Foie Gras as an appetizer is generally served sliced, with toast.

FONDELLI, FONDI (fohn-DAE-lee, FOHN-dee) *It.* Bottoms, or hearts of artichoke, CARCIOFO (kahr-CHOH-foh).

FONDS D'ARTICHAUT (fawn dar-tee-SHOH) *Fr.* Artichoke bottoms, or hearts of artichoke.

FONDUE (fawn-DEW) *Sw.* A Swiss specialty in which chunks of food are dipped into a pot of heated liquid and popped into the mouth—a dish for two or more. The name Fondue alone or Swiss

Fondue will mean cheese fondue, basically like Fondue Neuchâteloise, below. It is the custom that whoever loses his (her) chunk of bread in the fondue pot must pay the forfeit of a bottle of wine. (In some circles this is made a kissing forfeit.)

FONDUE BOURGUIGNONNE (boor-gee-NYAWN) This is beef fondue. Chunks of tender and lean raw beef are speared on long forks by the diners and plunged into a pot of hot oil on a spirit stove to brown, then dipped into an assortment of sauces, and popped into the mouth. The Burgundy in the name may refer to the Geneva region of Switzerland, which was once a part of Burgundy. But it might also be taken as a suggested liquid accompaniment.

FONDUE NEUCHÂTELOISE (nuh-shah-tel-WAHZ) Cheese fondue. This is a mixture of cheese, usually Emmenthal and Gruyère, melted in white wine, perhaps Neuchâteloise, with a touch of garlic, a little flour for thickening, a sprinkle of nutmeg, and laced with Kirsch. The diners dunk cubes of bread into the cheese mixture in the heated fondue pot. The crust of cheese that forms in the bottom of the pot should be cut into pieces so that everyone gets a taste.

FONDUTA (fohn-DOO-tah) *It.* A specialty of Piemonte (Piedmont). Melted Fontina cheese mixed with milk, egg yolk, a little butter, white pepper, and the famous white truffles of Piedmont, served with toast points for dipping.

FORESTIÈRE, À LA (faw-res-TYAER) *Fr.* Forest ranger style—that is, made with diced lean bacon, (morel) mushrooms, and potatoes cooked in butter.

FORMAGGIO (fohr-MAHJ-joh) *It.* Cheese.

FORNO, AL (FOHR-noh) *It.* Baked, roasted in the oven.

FOUR, AU (oh foor) *Fr.* "Into the oven"—baked, roasted.

FRA DIAVOLO (frah DYAH-voh-loh) *It.* A style of preparing lobster, ARAGOSTA (ah-rah-GOH-stah), and sometimes other shellfish, which is cut up and sautéed, often in its shell, and covered with a sauce made up of onions, garlic, olive oil, white wine, and tomatoes, and spiced with chopped parsley, oregano, and crushed dried red pepper. The hot pepper is often toned down, or completely left out, in this country to cater to the supposed American taste for unseasoned food. This dish was named for the seventeenth-century outlaw chieftain and ex-monk who gained the title Fra Diavolo, "Brother Devil," for his vicious crimes. Perhaps the hot, spicy nature of the dish suggested the connection with the devilish brigand.

FRAGOLE (FRAH-goh-lae) *It.* Strawberries.

FRAÎCHE, FRAIS (fresh, frae) *Fr.* Fresh, cool.
CRÈME FRAÎCHE (krem) Not just fresh cream; this is a double-thick heavy cream.

FRAISES (fraez) *Fr.* Strawberries; also a colorless eau-de-vie or fruit brandy made from strawberries.
FRAISES DE BOIS (duh bwah) Wild, forest strawberries.

FRAMBOISE (frahn-BWAHZ) *Fr.* Raspberries; also a colorless eau-de-vie or fruit brandy made from raspberries.

FRANCESE (frahn-CHAE-zae) *It.* In the French style as interpreted by the Italians. That is, dipped into a light batter of flour and egg, or (better) egg white, and sautéed; seasoned and/or garnished with lemon.

FREDDO (FRAED-doh) *It.* Cold.

FRENCH LAMB CHOPS Rib chops of lamb which have been "frenched"—that is, trimmed of the fat

45

and the thin strip of meat at the end of the bone. This bare bone is sometimes modestly covered with a paper frill.

FRENCH ONION SOUP Soupe à l'Oignon, which see (under Oignon).

FRESCO, FRESCHE (FRAE-skoh, FRAE-skae) *It.* Cool, fresh; uncooked.

FRICANDEAU (free-kan-DOH) *Fr.* A thick slice of meat, usually veal, studded with bacon or pork fat and braised in its own gravy; wine is sometimes added.

FRICASSÉE (free-ka-SAE) *Fr.* A method of stewing white meat or chicken. It is lightly browned with flavoring vegetables such as onions, carrots, perhaps celery, and chopped parsley, and stewed in water or broth, which is thickened with a flour-butter paste, sometimes cream, and may be seasoned with a few drops of lemon juice.

FRIT, FRITES (free, freet) *Fr.* Fried, sometimes deep fried.

FRITTO (FREET-toh) *It.* Fried or deep fried.

FRITTO MISTO (FREET-toh MEE-stoh) *It.* Mixed fry—breaded, floured or battered (coated with a flour-egg batter, that is) meat, poultry, and vegetables deep-fried in olive oil or, occasionally, clarified butter. The list of goodies includes scallops of veal, baby lamb chops, calf's liver, chicken, sweetbreads, kidneys, marrow, brains, rice croquettes, fritters, artichokes, mushrooms, zucchini, cauliflower buds, and much more. A variety from these, and other foods, may be used.

FRITTO MISTO DI MARE (dee MAH-rae) A mixed fry of the sea, or of seafood, also called FRITTO MISTO DI PESCE (dee PAE-shae).

FRITTURA MISTA (freet-TOO-rah MEE-stah) *It.* Same as Fritto Misto, which see.

FROID, FROIDE (frwah, frwahd) *Fr.* Cold.

FROMAGE (fraw-MAHZH) *Fr.* Cheese.

PLATEAU DE FROMAGE (pla-TOH duh) The cheese tray, an assortment of cheeses from which you may choose one or more kind(s).

FROMAGE DE TÊTE (fraw-MAHZH duh TAET) *Fr.* Headcheese.

FRUITS DE MER (frwee duh maer) *Fr.* "Fruits of the sea," seafood.

FRUTTA DI MARE (FROOT-tah dee MAH-rae) *It.* Literally, fruits of the sea, seafood.

FUMÉ (few-MAE) *Fr.* Smoked.

FUNGHI (FOON-gee) *It.* Mushrooms, Hobbit delicacy.

GAELIC COFFEE See Irish coffee.

GALANTINA, GALANTINE (gah-lahn-TEE-nah) *It.* (ga-lahn-TEEN) *Fr.* An elegant roll of stuffed poultry, especially chicken. The bird is boned, stuffed with ground meat, spices, and brandy, often thin strips of ham, chicken, veal or pork, and pork fat, sometimes truffles, and rolled up and cooked in a broth or bouillon with seasoning vegetables, herbs, and spices. Then it is cooled, sometimes decorated with aspic, and served cold, sliced.

GAMBERI, GAMBERETTI (GAHM-bae-ree, gahm-bae-RAET-tee) *It.* Shrimp, or, sometimes, crayfish. Gamberi are bigger, Gamberetti, smaller.

GARNI, GARNIE (gar-NEE) *Fr.* Garnished, with the trimmings. Garnishes may be simple or elaborate food additions, often vegetables, served with the meat, fish, poultry, etc., of the main dish.

GÂTEAU (gah-TOH) *Fr.* Cake.

GAZPACHO or GAZPACHO ANDALUZ (gahth-PAH-choh ahn-dah-LOOTH) *Sp.* A cold Andalusian soup—sometimes referred to as a salad soup—

47

made from raw diced tomatoes, cucumbers, sweet peppers, onions, water, bread, olive oil, and a little vinegar, seasoned with garlic, pepper, and sometimes a bit of cumin. Sometimes toasted bread is served separately.

GELATO (jae-LAH-toh) *It.* Ice cream.

GELÉE, EN (ahn zhu-LAE) *Fr.* Jellied, in aspic.

GENIÈVRE (zhu-NYAEVR) *Fr.* Juniper berries (the ones that give gin its distinctive flavor).

GENOISE (zheh-NWAHZ) *Fr.* Sponge cake.

GENOVESE, ALLA (je-noh-VAE-zae) *It.* Prepared in the style of Genoa (Genova), which is characterized by the use of aromatic herbs, especially basil.

GNOCCHI ALLA GENOVESE (NYOHK-kee) Potato dumplings in a sauce of fresh basil, olive oil, garlic, and grated cheese.

MINESTRONE ALLA GENOVESE (mee-nae-STROH-nae) Vegetable soup seasoned with fresh basil, very similar to the French Pistou.

RAVIOLI ALLA GENOVESE (rah-VYOH-lee) Little pockets of pasta filled with a variety of stuffings and eaten with sauce or in a broth. A specialty of Genoa, and describing them as Genovese may indicate just that, rather than the stuffing or the sauce.

GIBIER (zhih-BYAE) *Fr.* Game.

GIGOT (zhih-GOH) *Fr.* Leg of lamb or mutton.

GIORNO, DEL (dael JOHR-noh) *It.* "Of the day," as in soup of the day, specialty of the day.

GIROLLES, AUX (oh zhee-RAWL) *Fr.* Prepared with the wild yellow chanterelle mushrooms.

GUIDEA or GIUDIA, ALLA (joo-DAE-ah, joo-DEE-ah) *It.* Jewish style; a method of preparing artichokes, CARCIOFI (kahr-CHOH-fee). The dish is believed to have been invented by Abraham

Piperno, owner of a kosher restaurant in Rome over a century ago. Whole chokeless artichokes are flattened out and deep fried in olive oil until they are a deep bronze color and shaped like an open flower.

GLACÉ (gla-SAE) *Fr.* Iced, glazed, or candied.

GLACES (glas) *Fr.* Ice cream, ices.

GNOCCHI (NYOHK-kee) *It.* Dumplings made of flour, in some places also bread crumbs, milk, eggs. Parmesan cheese, and a touch of nutmeg; or of potato, DI PATATE (dee pah-TAH-tae), puréed and mixed with flour, eggs, and butter. Served topped with butter and grated cheese, tomato sauce, etc.

GNOCCHI VERDI (VAER-dee) Green gnocchi, made with spinach and Ricotta cheese, flour, eggs, milk; often served with just butter and grated Parmesan cheese.

GOULASH (GOO-lahsh) *Hng.* "Herdsman's" stew, or as they say, Gulyás. A stew with many variations, made with meat, usually beef, cooked with onions, tomato, sweet peppers, and potatoes, usually seasoned with caraway seeds and paprika. Sour cream is often stirred in.

GRANCHIO (GRAHN-kyoh) *It.* Crab.

GRAND DUC (grahn dewk) *Fr.* Prepared with a garnish of asparagus and truffles.

GRAND MARNIER (grahn mar-NYAE) An orange-based liqueur.

GRAND-MÈRE (grahn-MAER) *Fr.* Grandmother's style—that is, sautéed in butter and cooked with, or served with, mushrooms sautéed with bacon, glazed onions, and perhaps tiny potatoes, wine, a touch of Madeira, and seasoned with herbs such as bay leaf, thyme, and parsley. Grandma didn't fool around.

GRAND VENEUR (grahn vu-NUHR) *Fr.* In the style of the master of the hounds. A sauce for game—what else?—especially venison, VENAISON (vu-nae-ZAWn), which is made from red wine, wine vinegar, game broth, pepper, herbs such as parsley, thyme, bay leaf, perhaps rosemary or clove, seasoning vegetables such as carrots, onion, and/or shallots, thickened with a little flour and blended with cream and red currant jelly.

GRANITE (grah-NEE-tae) *It.* Water ices, like sherbet, but grainier—flavored with sweetened fruit juices.

GRAS-DOUBLE (gra-DOOBL) *Fr.* Tripe, but not the honeycomb type.

GRASSI (GRAHS-see) *It.* Fat, rich.

GRASSO, DI (dee GRAHS-soh) *It.* With meat, as opposed to the meatless version of a dish.

GRATIN, AU (oh gra-TAn) *Fr.* Baked with a crust of bread crumbs or bread crumbs with grated cheese; it has come to mean also with a crust of grated cheese, without the crumbs.

GRATINÉE (gra-tee-NAE) *Fr.* Same as au Gratin; also, a shorthand term for Onion Soup au Gratin, SOUPE À L'OIGNON GRATINÉE (soop ah law-NYAWn), which see under Oignon, Soup à l'.

GRATINATE (grah-tee-NAH-tae) *It.* Same as au Gratin, which see.

GRECQUE, À LA (grek) *Fr.* In the Greek style, as interpreted by the French. This is a method of preparing vegetables—mushrooms, artichoke hearts, cucumbers, etc.—as a cold hors d'oeuvre. The vegetable is boiled and cooled, and served in a sauce made with olive oil, water, sometimes also white wine, seasoned with lemon juice or vinegar and herbs such as thyme, bay leaf, and coriander.

GREEK SALAD, *Gk.* The traditional Greek salad,

called sometimes "country salad" or "peasant salad," is made with a variety of salad greens mixed with chunks of Féta cheese, black olives, anchovy fillets, with a dressing of olive oil, lemon juice, garlic, and herbs such as oregano and mint. Tomatoes are also frequently included, and other vegetables such as cucumber, and perhaps sweet peppers and green onions.

GREEN GODDESS A salad dressing from California, with a base of mayonnaise, sometimes sour cream, flavored with tarragon or tarragon vinegar, and other seasonings such as parsley, chives, anchovy, garlic, mustard, and pepper.

GREEN MAYONNAISE Mayonnaise greened with a purée of spinach, parsley, tarragon, watercress, chervil, and chives, or most of these.

GREEN SAUCE This is Green Mayonnaise, which see.

GRENADIN (gru-na-DAN) *Fr.* A small slice of veal studded with pork fat.

GRENOBLOISE, À LA (gru-noh-BLWAHZ) *Fr.* Garnished with capers and lemon slices, and sprinkled with chopped parsley.

GRENOUILLE (gru-NUHY) *Fr.* Frog; in restaurants, the frogs' legs.

GRIBICHE (gree-BEESH) *Fr.* A sauce for cold fish or shellfish. Oil and vinegar, or sometimes mayonnaise, mixed with pounded hard-boiled egg yolks, chopped gherkins, and capers, seasoned with herbs such as tarragon and chervil, and garnished with strips of hard-boiled egg whites.

GRIGLIA, ALLA (GREE-lyah) *It.* Grilled.

GRISSINI (grees-SEE-nee) *It.* Breadsticks, a specialty of Turin (Torino).

GUACAMOLE (gwah-kah-MOH-lae) *Mx.* Mashed avocado mixed with minced onion and tomatoes, hot chili peppers, a little coriander or perhaps parsley. To spread on tortillas or as a side dish.

GUMBO A Creole specialty; from the French word for okra, "gombo." A soup of chicken, ham or bacon, or shellfish (crab, shrimp, oysters), or all three, cooked with okra, onions, tomatoes, celery, perhaps green peppers, and rice, and seasonings such as thyme, bay leaf, parsley, and hot pepper, thickened with a paste of flour and butter or oil browned together.

FILÉ GUMBO (fee-lae) is thickened with filé powder—made from sassafras leaves (root beer is made from the roots of the same tree). It was the Choctaw Indians who first made the powder and introduced it to the Creole French in Louisiana.

HACHÉ (a-SHAE) *Fr.* Chopped up, or sliced.

HALF-SHELL, ON THE When shellfish is described simply as "on the half-shell," it will be served raw, usually with lemon wedges and a cocktail sauce; see Cocktail, Seafood.

HARENG (ar-AHɴ) *Fr.* Herring.

HARICOTS VERTS (a-ree-KOH VAER) *Fr.* String beans, French beans.

HASENPFEFFER (HAH-zen-fef-fer) *Gm.* Hare stew. The hare is sautéed and stewed in red wine and bouillon, sometimes with onion, and seasoned with herbs such as parsley, thyme, bay leaf, perhaps also a dash of lemon juice, and sometimes a grating of chocolate. It is served with red currant jelly.

HAY AND STRAW See Paglia e Fieno.

HEADCHEESE Cheese it's not, but it does come from the head—and feet, and other bits and pieces—of the pig or calf. These meat trimmings are boiled with onions and herbs (often marjoram, sage, nutmeg or cloves, and pepper) and cooled in

52

this broth, which jells around it. It is sliced, and served often with a Vinaigrette or mustard sauce.

HÉLÈNE (ae-LEN) *Fr.* A style of preparing pears, POIRE (pwahr), or perhaps other fruit, which are poached and served over vanilla ice cream and topped with chocolate sauce, or with the chocolate sauce on the side.

HENRI IV (ahn-REE KATR) *Fr.* Garnished with artichoke bottoms filled with a sauce of egg yolk and butter, flavored with shallots and tarragon, sometimes chervil, and a touch of wine vinegar. This is Béarnaise Sauce, named in honor of Henri IV, who came from Béarn.

HOCHEPOCHE, HOCHEPOT (awsh-PAWSH, awsh-POH) *Fr.* A stew made with a hodgepodge of meats—beef (often oxtail), pig's feet, veal or mutton, and sausages—cooked with mixed vegetables such as cabbage, turnip, carrots, onions, leeks and celery, and seasonings.

HOLLANDAISE (aw-lahn-DAEZ) *Fr.* A French sauce of Dutch origin; a rich sauce of egg yolks, butter, lemon juice or vinegar, and a little pepper.

HOLSTEIN, À LA or HOLSTEINERSCHNITZEL See under Schnitzel.

HOMARD (aw-MAR) *Fr.* Lobster.

HONGROISE, À LA (awn-GRWAHZ) *Fr.* Hungarian style—that is, made with paprika and cream, usually sour cream.

HORS-D'OEUVRE (awr-DUHVR) *Fr.* An appetizer or a tidbit served before the meal.

HORSEBACK, ANGELS ON, *Br.* These angels are oysters, their horses—pieces of toast. The oysters are wrapped in slices of bacon, sometimes squirted with lemon juice, and broiled; served on pieces of buttered toast.

HÔTELIÈRE (oh-tel-YAER) *Fr.* "Innkeeper's style":

served with melted butter, chopped parsley, lemon juice, and sautéed mushrooms.

HUILE, À L' (a lweel) *Fr.* In oil.

POMMES DE TERRE À L'HUILE (pawm duh taer) French potato salad; boiled potatoes, cut up and dressed with white wine, oil and vinegar, a touch of mustard, and often chopped scallions or shallots and parsley.

HUÎTRES (hweetr) *Fr.* Oysters.

HUSH PUPPIES A specialty of the southern United States—deep-fried dough balls made with cornmeal, flour, egg, baking powder, and milk or buttermilk, sometimes a bit of grated onion. The peculiar name comes, or so they say, from one of their uses—being thrown to the dogs to stop their yapping.

IMPÉRIALE, À L' (an-pae-RYAL) *Fr.* Served with a garnish of truffles, foie gras, cockscombs, kidneys, and similar delicacies.

INDIENNE, À L' (an-DYEN) *Fr.* Indian style—that is, curried; with curry sauce; often garnished with rice.

INDIVIA (een-DEE-vyah) *It.* Endive.

INGLESE, ALL' (een-GLAE-zae) *It.* English style. A method of preparing calf's liver, FEGATO DI VITELLO (FAE-gah-toh dee vee-TAEL-loh), which is sautéed with bacon.

SOGLIOLA INGLESE (SOH-lyoh-lah) This is simply English sole, Dover sole.

ZUPPA INGLESE (DZOOP-pah) This "English soup" is no soup, nor is it English. This is a dessert of Italian invention—sponge cake in layers spread with custard is soused—did I say "soused"? I meant "doused"—in rum and/or liqueur. The slice of cake is topped with more custard, then meringue or whipped cream, and sometimes studded with candied fruits.

INSALATA (een-sah-LAH-tah) *It.* Salad.

INSALATA DI MARE or DI PESCE (dee MAH-rae, PAE-shae) Seafood salad; assorted shellfish—shrimp, squid, scallops, clams or mussels, perhaps crab or lobster—and sometimes fish, are cooked, cooled, and served in a dressing of oil and lemon juice or vinegar, garlic, and parsley.

INVOLTINI (een-vohl-TEE-nee) *It.* Literally, little wrapped-up bundles. This is a thin slice of meat—veal, if not otherwise specified—rolled up around a filling, braised, and served with a sauce.

IRISH COFFEE Black coffee sweetened with sugar, and laced with Irish whiskey, with whipped cream or perhaps thick, heavy cream floated on the top.

IRISH STEW *Ir.* A traditional Irish dish, made with mutton or lamb, thickly sliced potatoes, and onions stewed in water and seasoned with a little thyme.

JAMBALAYA (jum-bu-LAH-yu) A Creole specialty; a stew or casserole of rice with shrimp, ham, and sometimes chicken, and/or a peppery sausage, cooked in a broth with onion, garlic, often tomatoes, celery, green peppers and pimientos, and seasoned with bay leaf, parsley, thyme, and usually chili powder.

JAMBON (zhahn-BAWɴ) *Fr.* Ham.

JARDINIÈRE (zhar-dee-NYAER) *Fr.* Gardener's style; a garnish for meat or poultry, which is surrounded by fresh vegetables in little homogeneous groups—glazed turnips and carrots, string beans, peas, kidney beans, sometimes cauliflower buds.

JEREZ (he-RETH) *Sp.* Sherry.

JOUR, DU (dew zhoor) *Fr.* Of the day, as in the

soup, SOUPE (soop), of the day; the dish, PLAT (pla), of the day; or vegetable, LÉGUME (lae-GEWM), of the day.

JUBILÉE (zhew-bee-LAE) *Fr.* A festive preparation for cherries, CERISES (su-REEZ), which are cooked in syrup, and served with flaming brandy or Kirsch (cherry brandy), often over vanilla ice cream.

JUGGED HARE, *Br.* A jug to the English is a stew of game cooked in an earthenware crock. In this case, hare stewed in red wine, with onion, mushrooms, celery, bacon, often a splash of brandy, and a touch of vinegar and/or lemon juice, garlic, carrots, a little thyme, bay leaf, perhaps allspice or juniper berries, and thickened with a little flour-butter paste and the hare's blood.

JULIENNE (zhew-LYEN) *Fr.* A style of cutting vegetables or meat—into a matchstick shape, or shreds. Also the name of a Consommé. Consommé Julienne (kawn-saw-MAE) is a clear soup or bouillon with shredded vegetables such as carrots, celery, turnips, leeks, cabbage, and lettuce which have been cooked in butter, and peas, and seasoned with chopped onions and chervil.

JUS, AU (oh zhew) *Fr.* In its own natural juices.

KABOBS, KEBABS (ku-BAWBS) *Trk.* Chunks of meat, often marinated meat, skewered and broiled or grilled, and generally basted with a spicy sauce. SHISH-KEBAB A Turkish specialty of lamb or mutton grilled on a skewer. The meat chunks are marinated in or basted with a mixture of olive oil, lemon juice, herbs, and spices such as cinnamon and allspice. The meat is skewered alternately with pieces of onion, sometimes also mushrooms, green pepper, and tomato. Sometimes done with a tomato sauce. Shish-kebab is often served with rice pilaf.

KASSELER RIPPCHEN or RIPPENSPEER (KAHZ-ler RIHP-shen, RIHP-pen-shpaer) *Gm.* Smoked pork chops or loin of pork, respectively. The meat is roasted or boiled, and served with sauerkraut or red cabbage, ROTKOHL (ROHT-kohl).

KEY LIME PIE A dessert of the Florida Keys. A pie filled with a chilled mixture of sweetened milk, lime juice, and grated lime rind, and topped with meringue (egg whites whipped with sugar).

KEBABS See Kabobs.

KIEV, À LA (KEE-ev) *Rs.* A preparation for chicken breasts in the style of the city of Kiev (Kotelety po Kievski). The skinned and boned chicken meat, sometimes pounded flat, is stuffed with a filling of butter mixed with seasonings such as parsley, chives, garlic, shallots, and/or green onions. The cutlets are coated with flour, egg, and bread crumbs and sautéed in butter or oil.

KING, À LA A style of preparing chicken. Often served on toast. Cubed chicken in a sauce made with cream or milk, sometimes egg yolk, and chicken broth, seasoned with a dash of lemon juice, paprika, and a little Sherry, with chopped green and red peppers, onions, mushrooms, and sometimes peas. This dish was created at the turn of the century by chef George Greenwald at the Brighton Beach Hotel on Long Island, New York, for E. Clarke King II.

KIPPERED HERRING, KIPPERS, *Br.* Split herring, mildly salted and smoked to a coppery hue.

KIRSCH (keersh) A fruit brandy made from black cherries.

KÖNIGSBERGER KLOPS (KUH-nihgz-baer-ger

klawps) *Gm.* Meatballs in the style of Königsberg, the former capital of East Prussia; made with beef and pork, bread, egg, onions, capers, and anchovies. They are poached, and served in a gravy seasoned with bay leaf, cloves, perhaps allspice, lemon juice, capers, and anchovies, and thickened with flour.

KOULIBIAC (koo-lee-BYAHK), KULIBIAKA (koo-lee-BYAH-kah,) *Rs.* Russian fish pie filled with layers of fish fillets—often salmon—onion, seasonings, sliced hard-boiled eggs, kasha (buckwheat) or rice, and chopped vesiga (sturgeon marrow) in a sauce of melted butter, and topped with a crust brushed with egg.

LAIT (lae) *Fr.* Milk.

LAITUE (lae-TEW)) *Fr.* Lettuce.

LAMPONI (lahm-POH-nee) *It.* Raspberries.

LANGOUSTE (lahn-GOOST) *Fr.* Spiny (rock) lobster.

LANGOUSTINES (lahn-goo-STEEN) *Fr.* Saltwater crayfish, Dublin Bay Prawns.

LANGUE (lahng) *Fr.* Tongue.

LAPEREAU, LAPIN (la-PROH, la-PAɴ) *Fr.* Rabbit.

LARD, LARDON (lar, lar-DAWɴ) *Fr.* Bacon; a strip of bacon.

LASAGNE (lah-ZAH-nyae) *It.* Squares of pasta or very wide noodles, sometimes made with spinach purée, VERDE (VAER-dae). Lasagne is baked, AL FORNO (ahl FOHR-noh), generally with meat or tomato sauce, and Ricotta cheese mixed with egg or a cream sauce, and topped with a crust of grated cheese or perhaps strips of browned Mozzarella cheese.

LATTE (LAH-tae) *It.* Milk.

LATTUGA (laht-TOO-gah) *It.* Lettuce.

LÉGUMES, LEGUMI (lae-GEWM) *Fr.* (lae-GOO-mee) *It.* Vegetables.

LEMON SOLE A variety of sole; no connection to the citrus fruit.

LENTICCHIE (laen-TEEK-kyae) *It.* Lentils.

LEPRE (LAE-prae) *It.* Hare.

LESSATO, LESSO (laes-SAH-toh, LAES-soh) *It.* Boiled.

LIÈGEOISE, À LA (lyae-ZHWAHZ) *Bg.* A dish described as in the style of Liège will be prepared with the juniper berries for which this Belgian city is famous.

LIÈVRE (lyaevr) *Fr.* Hare.

LIMONE (lee-MOH-nae) *It.* Lemons.

LIMOUSINE, À LA (lee-moo-ZEEN) *Fr.* Dishes made in this style will generally be garnished with red cabbage braised with chestnuts.

LINGUA (LEEN-gwah) *It.* Tongue.

LINGUINE (leen-GWEE-nae) *It.* Narrow ribbon pasta; "little tongues"?

LITTLE NECKS Small, hard-shelled clams, or quahogs; the smallest size. Generally served raw, on the half-shell.

LIVORNESE (lee-vohr-NAE-zae) *It.* Prepared in the style of Livorno, or Leghorn. Generally seafood, which is cooked in oil with tomato, garlic, celery, often olives and capers, and perhaps anchovies, seasoned with chopped parsley.

LONGE (lawnzh) *Fr.* Loin.

LOUIS, CRAB A West Coast crabmeat salad; other shellfish may be prepared in the same style. The crabmeat is tossed with a cold sauce of mayonnaise mixed with whipped cream, a little chili sauce, grated onion, chopped parsley, a squirt of lemon juice, and a dash of hot cayenne pepper.

May be served on lettuce, garnished with black olives and/or hard-boiled eggs.

LUCIANA (loo-CHAH-nah) *It.* A light sauce of white wine, olive oil, and tomatoes, seasoned with garlic and parsley.

LUMACHE (loo-MAH-kae) *It.* Snails.

LYONNAISE (lyohn-NAEZ) *Fr.* When you see a dish prepared in the style of Lyons, you can count on its being made with onions; usually, onions sautéed in butter, and often made into a sauce with white wine, the juice of the meat it accompanies (if any), and sometimes a touch of vinegar.

SAUCISSONS LYONNAIS or DE LYON (soh-see-SAWN lyohn-NAE, duh LYOHn) Lyon sausage is served sliced, uncooked. It is made of pork, studded with dices of pork fat and white peppercorns, and seasoned with salt, pepper, and a little garlic. It is dried, SEC (sek), that is, cured by drying.

MAATJES HERRING (MAHT-ches) *Ht.* Dutch herring, lightly salted; called Maatjes (virgin) because only the very young female herring are used for this type of curing.

MACÉDOINE DE FRUITS, MACEDONIA DI FRUTTA (ma-sae-DWAHN duh FRWEE) *Fr.* (mah-chae-DOH-nyah dee FROOT-tah) *It.* This is a mixture of cut-up fruits in syrup and liqueur, often Kirsch or Maraschino. May also be served in aspic, but not commonly.

MÂCONNAISE, À LA (mah-kaw-NAEZ) *Fr.* A dish prepared in the style of the wine-producing region of Mâcon will be prepared with red wine. Sole Mâconnaise is poached in red wine.

MADEIRA (mah-DE-ru) A Portuguese wine fortified by the addition of brandy.

60

MADÈRE (ma-DAER) *Fr.* A sauce of rich meat broth flavored with Madeira.

MADRILÈNE (ma-drih-LEN) *Fr.* Madrid consommé; beef consommé flavored and colored with tomatoes; seasoned with leeks or chives, sometimes tarragon and parsley, and a dash of Port. Generally served cold.

MAGENTA (mah-JAEN-tah) *It.* A style of preparing veal cutlets, COSTOLETTA (koh-stoh-LAET-tah). They are stuffed with Prosciutto, cheese, and paté.

MAGRO, DI (dee MAH-groh) *It.* "Lean," of meat; or "meatless," as in Lenten dishes.

MAIALE (mah-YAH-lae) *It.* Pork. How this came to be the word for pork goes back to Roman times. The Romans offered the sacrifice of a pig at the altar of the goddess Maia.

MAIGRE, AU (oh maegr) *Fr.* Prepared without meat.

MAINTENON (mant-NAWN) *Fr.* Prepared with a cream sauce thickened with egg yolks and flavored with onion and mushrooms.

MAÏS (ma-EES) *Fr.* Corn.

MAISON, À LA (mae-ZAWN) *Fr.* Prepared in the style of the house.

MAÎTRE D'HÔTEL (maetr doh-TEL) *Fr.* Maître d' style; prepared with a sauce of butter creamed with lemon juice, chopped parsley, and a sprinkle of pepper.

MANCHE, DE LA (duh la mahnsh) *Fr.* Sole described as "of the channel" is, of course, Dover sole of the English Channel.

MANDARINE (mahn-da-REEN) *Fr.* Tangerine or mandarin orange.

MANDORLE (MAHN-dohr-lae) *It.* Almonds.

MANHATTAN STYLE When speaking of .chow-

61

der, this means it's made with tomatoes rather than milk—which would be New England style.

MANICOTTI (mah-nee-KOHT-tee) *It.* These "muffs" are sometimes stuffed tubes of pasta but more frequently squares of pasta rolled up around a filling of meat or cheese. In this country, it's usually a filling of Ricotta cheese mixed with egg, grated Parmesan, and seasoned with a sprinkle of nutmeg and chopped parsley. The rolls of pasta are topped with a cream and/or tomato sauce.

MANZO (MAHN-dzoh) *It.* Beef.

MAQUEREAU (ma-KROH) *Fr.* Mackerel.

MARASCHINO A liqueur made from fermented Marasca cherries.

MARCHAND DE VIN (mar-SHAHn duh VAn) *Fr.* A dish prepared with the wine merchant's sauce has a sauce of shallots cooked in concentrated red wine and meat broth, to which butter, pepper, a dash of lemon juice, and a sprinkling of parsley are added.

MARÉCHALE, À LA (ma-re-SHAL) *Fr.* Field marshal style; dipped in egg and bread crumbs and fried in butter; served garnished with asparagus tips and truffle slices, classically.

MARECHIARO (mah-rae-KYAH-roh) *It.* In the style of Marechiaro, a fishing village in the Bay of Naples—in a sauce of olive oil, white wine, garlic, tomato, and parsley, basil, or oregano.

MARENGO A French-Italian preparation for chicken originally, but now also for veal. The meat is sautéed in olive oil and cooked in a sauce of white wine, tomatoes, garlic, Cognac, sometimes mushrooms, black olives, and onions, and topped with crayfish or shrimp. The seafood, though, is frequently left out. Traditionally it is served with a fried egg on the side. I say French-Italian because the dish was created by a French chef, but the ingredients were determined, according to the story, by the area of Italy where he happened to be at the time. (It can be found in restaurants in both countries.) It seems that after Napoleon's victory over the Austrians at Marengo in 1800, the famished hero ordered his dinner to be served "tout de suite." His chef, Dunand the Younger, had to come up with a suitable meal from whatever ingredients he could quickly lay his hands on. The best he could scout up in the immediate vicinity was four tomatoes, three eggs, some garlic, olive oil, a scrawny chicken, and a few crayfish. Just this, and a single pan to cook it in. The inventive chef cut up the bird with his sword, fried it in the oil with the garlic and the eggs, and added the tomatoes and a little water laced with some of Napoleon's own brandy for a sauce. Feeling perhaps that this was none too much for the general's victory dinner, he popped the crayfish into the pan as well. He served the dish with his army ration of bread, and not without some misgivings. Napoleon, however, was so pleased with the dish that he ordered it served him after every battle. It is said that Dunand later decided to improve on the original dish by putting in mushrooms in place of the unorthodox crayfish, but Napoleon took one look at it and demanded to know where his crayfish were. That had been his victory dinner at Marengo, and apparently he wanted to stick with a winner.

MARGUERY (mar-gu-REE) *Fr.* A style of preparing fish, especially sole, which is poached with mussels and shrimp and served in a rich sauce made from the wine in which the fish was poached, reduced, and thickened with egg yolks and butter. Named for the Paris restaurant where it was created.

MARINARA, ALLA (mah-ree-NAH-rah) *It.* Sailor style. This is a dish, usually fish, but sometimes pasta, prepared with a sauce of oil, garlic, chopped tomatoes, parsley, and/or oregano.

MARINATO (mah-ree-NAH-toh) *It.* Marinated, pickled.

MARINÉ (ma-ree-NAE) *Fr.* Pickled, soused.

MARINIÈRE (ma-ree-NYAER) *Fr.* Sailor style; a style of preparing seafood, especially mussels, MOULES (mool), which are steamed in their shells in white wine, a little chopped onion or shallots cooked in oil or butter, and seasoned with thyme, bay leaf, chopped parsley, and a sprinkle of pepper. French bread is often served with this dish for sopping up the sauce.

MARMITE or PETITE MARMITE (pu-TEET mar-MEET) *Fr.* A Parisian soup named for the pot it's traditionally made in. Big or small (petite), this is a soup of beef, marrow bones, chicken, chicken giblets, leeks, celery, onions, carrots, turnip and cabbage, seasoned with parsley, thyme, and bay leaf, and perhaps a couple of cloves. In the French manner, the broth is served with the vegetables in the Marmite, and the meat and the chicken are cut up and re-added to the soup at the table. Toast sprinkled with grated cheese, or sometimes spread with the marrow, is floated in the soup.

MARRONI, MARRONS (mahr-ROH-nee) *It.* (ma-RAWN) *Fr.* Chestnuts.

MARSALA, AL (mahr-SAH-lah) *It.* A style of preparing veal cutlets, SCALOPPINE (skah-lohp-PEE-nae), which are flattened with a cutlet bat, dusted with flour, sometimes sprinkled with lemon juice, and sautéed in butter and olive oil. A sauce made from Marsala, and perhaps a little meat broth, added to the butter and reduced to a syrupy glaze is poured over the cutlets. Marsala is an Italian, or Sicilian to be more precise, fortified wine, usually sweet.

MARYLAND CHICKEN Fried or baked chicken as it is made Maryland-style is salted and peppered, dipped into flour, egg, and milk, and rolled in bread crumbs, and cooked in fat. It is served topped with a gravy made from the pan drippings mixed with flour and milk.

MASCOTTE, MASCOTTI (mas-KAWT) *Fr.* (mah-SKOHT-tee) *It.* A style of preparing meat or poultry, which is served in a white wine sauce made with the meat (or poultry) broth, with hearts of artichoke, mushrooms or tiny potato balls cooked in butter, and truffle slices.

MATELOTE (ma-TLOHT) *Fr.* A stew of freshwater fish and/or eels in the style of the sailor's wife. The fish and/or eels are stewed in wine, often red wine, with little onions, garlic, and mushrooms cooked in butter, seasoned with bay leaf, thyme, and parsley, and thickened with a flour-butter paste.

MATJES HERRING (MAHT-ches) Young, salted herring.

MATRICIANA, ALLA See Amatriciana, all'.

MEDAGLIONE (mae-dah-LYOH-nae) *It.* Medallions, small round slices, usually thick slices, of meat, fish, or sometimes paté or other composed foods.

MÉDAILLON (mae-da-YAWɴ) *Fr.* Same as Medaglione, which see.

MELANZANE (mae-lahn-DZAH-nae) *It.* Eggplant.

MELBA, PÊCHE (pehsh) *Fr.* An ice cream dessert invented in 1892 by Escoffier in honor of Dame Nellie Melba, the famous Australian soprano: peaches steeped in vanilla syrup on a bed of vanilla ice cream, topped with raspberry syrup or purée.

MELE (MAE-lae) *It.* Apples.

MERINGUE GLACÉE (mu-RAnG gla-SAE) *Fr.* Ice cream topped with meringue—a froth of egg whites beaten with sugar.

MEUNIÈRE (muhn-YAER) *Fr.* In the style of the miller's wife. A method of cooking fish, which is dusted with flour, and fried in butter till golden. The butter is seasoned with chopped parsley and a dash of lemon juice and poured over the fish.

MIEL, MIELE (myel) *Fr.* (MYAE-lae) *It.* Honey.

MIGNON, FILET (fee-LAE mee-NYAWn) *Fr.* This "little fillet," from the tenderloin, is not very big around but quite thick.

MIGNONETTES (mee-nyaw-NET) *Fr.* Small slices of Filet Mignon.

MILANESE (mee-lah-NAE-zae) *It.* In general this means the way the dish is prepared in Milano. The dishes of this northern Italian city tend to be somewhat hearty.

COSTOLETTA ALLA MILANESE (koh-stoh-LAET-tah) This is a veal chop, flattened with a cutlet bat, dipped into beaten egg, bread crumbs, and sautéed in butter. It is served with lemon wedges. This is the prototype for the Wiener-erschnitzel, although the Viennese use a boneless cut of veal, and the Costoletta is a loin chop, traditionally on the bone.

MINESTRONE ALLA MILANESE (mee-nae-STROH-nae) Vegetable soup Milano style is made with rice in place of the usual pasta.

RISOTTO ALLA MILANESE (ree-ZOHT-toh) A dish of creamy rice, cooked in wine and meat broth and flavored with onion and bone marrow cooked in butter, gilded with saffron, and topped with grated Parmesan cheese.

MILLE-FEUILLE, MILLE FOGLIE (meel fuhy) *Fr.*

(MEEL-lae FOH-lyae) *It.* Literally, a thousand leaves; this is a rectangle of layered flaky puff pastry filled with fruit jam—sometimes spiked with fruit brandy or liqueur—and/or pastry cream: a light custard made from sugar, egg, milk, butter, and flavored with vanilla, coffee, or chocolate. The pastry is topped with confectioners' sugar or frosting.

MINCEMEAT A pie filling made of minced apples, raisins, currants, candied orange, lemon, and citron peel, beef suet (fat), sometimes beef, sugar (often brown sugar), and seasoned with mixed spices such as cinnamon, mace, clove, and nutmeg, lemon peel, and orange or lemon juice, and laced with brandy, rum, and/or Madeira. This used to be just what it says—minced meat, flavored with spices, but over the years some of the meat was replaced by dried fruit, and frequently the only vestige of the original minced meat is the suet.

MINESTRA (mee-NAE-strah) *It.* Soup, usually thick soup. The name is believed to come from the Latin word "ministrare"—to serve. And this was the dish that was served from the ever-ready kettle at the monasteries to the traveler who stopped over for an evening's lodging in the days before there were inns.

MINESTRONE (mee-nae-STROH-nae) *It.* This is a big Minestra; vegetable soup with pasta or rice. It generally doesn't contain any meat except for chopped bacon or salt pork, or a bit of ham or pork. Which vegetables will find their way into the pot depends on the season and the region of Italy where the recipe is from, but there will generally be white kidney beans, diced carrots, celery, garlic, and onions, shredded cabbage, chopped tomatoes or tomato paste, often diced zucchini, and green peas. Diced potatoes are not uncommon, and you may see chopped spinach and leeks. There will be pasta in one form or another, usually some small shape, or rice—especially if it's MINESTRONE ALLA MILANESE (mee-lah-NAE-zae). The soup may be made with beef or chicken broth, or simply water. Minestrone is commonly seasoned with parsley and basil, sometimes sage and/or thyme, and usually, if not always, sprinkled with grated Parmesan cheese, or the local variety, just before serving.

MINUTE STEAK   A very thin boneless steak which is broiled or sautéed in just a couple of minutes.

MIRABEAU (mee-ra-BOH) *Fr.* A garnish served usually with grilled meat. It is made up of anchovy fillets arranged in a crisscross pattern on the meat with pitted olives, blanched tarragon leaves, and anchovy butter. Named for the French revolutionary Mirabeau.

MIROTON DE BOEUF (mee-raw-TAWN duh BUHF) *Fr.* A preparation for slices of boiled beef or pot roast. The meat is reheated in a sauce made from sautéed onions, often a little vinegar, white wine and beef broth seasoned with tarragon, parsley, and perhaps a bit of tomato paste. Miroton is traditionally served in the dish it's been cooked in.

MISTO (MEE-stoh) *It.* Mixed.

MIXED GRILL, Br. A variety of broiled, or sometimes fried, meats including such types as lamb chops, calf's liver, rashers of bacon, sausages, kidneys, tenderloin steak, chopped steak, perhaps veal chops. It is often garnished with tomato and mushrooms.

MOCK TURTLE SOUP, *Br.* A clear soup in English cookery made to resemble turtle soup, but without the turtle. Calf's head makes the substitution. This is a rich clear soup made from meat broth flavored with stock-pot vegetables—carrots, onions, scallions, and celery, and seasoned with clove, bay leaf, parsley, thyme, and perhaps basil or marjoram, and laced with Madeira, Sherry, or Port. The soup is strained and served with chopped bits of boiled calf's head.

MODE, À LA (mawd) *Fr.* This simply means "in the style."

BOEUF À LA MODE (buhf) Pot roast of beef, traditionally studded with pork fat, braised in red wine laced with a bit of brandy and meat broth made with calf's feet, seasoned with onion (sometimes whole small onions), celery, carrots in chunks, and garlic, and spiced with thyme, bay leaf, parsley, allspice, and sometimes a piece of orange peel. A little Madeira or Port is often added. The beef is sometimes served cold in its own aspic, but more often hot, surrounded by the carrots, onions, if they were whole, and perhaps the calf's feet.

PIE À LA MODE   In America this means a piece of some variety of two-crust fruit pie served topped with a scoop or two of ice cream.

MOELLE, À LA (mwal) *Fr.* Prepared with bone marrow, usually in a brown sauce made with meat broth, white wine, chopped shallots cooked in butter, seasoned with a little thyme and bay leaf, and sprinkled with chopped parsley.

MOLECHE (moh-LAE-kae) *It.* Soft-shelled crabs, which are generally floured and sautéed in butter. You eat the whole thing, shell and all; it's that soft.

MONT BLANC, MONTE BIANCO (mawn blahn) *Fr.* (MOHN-tae BYAHN-koh) *It.* A "mountain" of puréed chestnuts which have been cooked in milk with sugar and vanilla, topped with a "snow cap" of vanilla-flavored whipped cream.

MONTMORENCY, À LA (mawn-maw-rahn-SEE) *Fr.* Any dish à la Montmorency is sure (or as sure as one can be with these things) to have cherries in its makeup. This is the name of a variety of tart cherry originally grown in a section of Paris.

CANARD À LA MONTMORENCY (ka-NAR) Broiled or roasted duck in a sauce made from its own broth and a little wine to which black cherries and perhaps a little Port are added.

MORILLES, AUX (oh maw-REEY) *Fr.* Prepared with the wild morel mushroom.

MORNAY (mawr-NAE) *Fr.* A cream sauce made up of butter and flour cooked with milk, broth, heavy cream, sometimes egg yolks, and grated cheese—usually Gruyère and Parmesan—and seasoned with a sprinkle of nutmeg.

MORUE (maw-REW) *Fr.* Dried salt cod.

MOULES (mool) *Fr.* Mussels.

MOUSSAKA (moo-sah-KAH) A Balkan casserole of eggplant fried in olive oil, layered with a mixture of sautéed onions and garlic, ground lamb—other meats are sometimes substituted—chopped tomatoes, red or white wine, and sometimes pine nuts, spiced with oregano, parsley, and nutmeg. In Greece it is topped with a cream sauce made with flour, butter, milk, and egg yolk. The casserole is dusted with grated Parmesan or the local hard cheese. In other countries it may be sprinkled with bread crumbs (in place of the cream sauce and cheese) or simply left plain. In Rumanian cookery the Moussaka is wrapped in the skins of the eggplant, purple side out. In this style, mushrooms are sometimes also included.

MOUSSE (moos) *Fr.* Literally, froth or foam; this is an airy dish with a velvety texture. Mousse may be a main dish, hot or cold, or a dessert, depending on the ingredients used. Mousse is made of a purée of meat, poultry, or fish, or of vegetables, fruit or sweets such as chocolate, CHOCOLAT (shaw-kaw-LA), which might be the most popular mousse. Mousses are fluffed up with beaten eggs and usually whipped cream. Most also contain butter, and those made of heavier ingredients such as meat may also incorporate gelatin to hold their shape. Mousse is often served molded.

MOUSSELINE (moos-LEEN) *Fr.* This term is used to describe dishes, hot or cold, enriched with whipped cream, such as Mousse for example. It is also the name of a sauce made of mayonnaise or Hollandaise to which whipped cream has been added.

MOUTARDE (moo-TARD) *Fr.* Mustard. Also a sauce made of Hollandaise—egg yolks, butter, and lemon juice or vinegar—highly spiced with mustard.

MOUTON (moo-TAWN) *Fr.* Mutton.

MOUX, CRABES (krab moo) *Fr.* Soft-shelled crabs, which are usually floured and sautéed in butter, often with almonds, AUX AMANDES (oh za-MAHnD) or AMANDINE (ah-mahn-DEEN). You can eat the whole thing, shell and all—it's that soft.

MUGNAIA (moo-NYAH-yah) *It.* Miller style, which means dusted with the miller's product—flour—and sautéed in butter, sprinkled with lemon juice and chopped parsley.

MUSCOLI (MOO-skoh-lee) *It.* Mussels.

NAGE, À LA (nazh) *Fr.* Literally, in swimming; a preparation for shellfish. Generally the swimmers are crayfish, ÉCREVISSES (ae-kru-VEES), or lobster, HOMARD (aw-MAR), which are cooked in a broth of white wine flavored with carrots, onions, shallots, and a little garlic, bay leaf, thyme, parsley, and perhaps a touch of hot cayenne pepper. The shellfish is served, hot or cold, along with the broth, which is drunk with it.

NANTUA (NAN-twah) *Fr.* A sauce made from crayfish butter—that is, crayfish purée creamed with butter and served mixed with butter and flour, cream, crayfish broth, sometimes white wine, a few drops of brandy, egg yolk, a little tomato, and a pinch of hot pepper. À LA NANTUA means garnished with crayfish or rock lobster tails and perhaps a purée of the shellfish.

NAPOLÉON, NAPOLEONE (na-paw-lae-AWn) *Fr.* (nah-poh-lae-OH-nae) *It.* A flaky pastry dessert which really has nothing to do with the French emperor, as far as we know. Flaky pastry, of which this is one type, was introduced to Europe by the Saracens. Napoléons are rectangles of flaky puff pastry in layers filled with a light custard or pastry cream made with eggs, sugar, milk, butter, and vanilla, or occasionally whipped cream. They may be topped with confectioners' sugar or with icing zigzagged with lines of chocolate.

NAPOLITAIN (na-paw-lee-TAn) *Fr.* Literally, Neapolitan—but in Naples it's called "Sfogliatelle." This is another name for the Napoléon, which see.

NATUR, AU NATUREL (na-TEWR, oh na-tewr-EL) *Fr.* Cooked very simply, plain, unadorned.

NAVARIN (na-va-RAn) *Fr.* A stew, or ragout, of mutton, DE MOUTON (duh moo-TAWn), or lamb, D'AGNEAU (da-NYOH). This stew may be cooked with a variety of vegetables, the simplest being onions and potatoes. Often the chunks of meat are browned with onions and carrots in fat, sprinkled with flour, and stewed in water or white wine with potatoes, seasoned with a clove of garlic and perhaps a little tomato, bay leaf, chopped parsley, and thyme.

NAVARIN PRINTANIER (pran-ta-NYAE) Mutton, or lamb, stew with spring vegetables—new potatoes, small onions, carrots and turnips in chunks, green peas and string beans; also flavored with chopped tomatoes and garlic, and the stock-pot herbs.

NEIGE, OEUFS À LA (uh za la naezh) *Fr.* Egg-shaped puffs of meringue (egg whites beaten with sugar) poached in sweetened milk and served, cold, in a dish of custard made of milk, egg yolks, and sugar, and flavored with vanilla. These "snow eggs" are sometimes called Floating Islands.

NESSELRODE *Fr.* A rich, molded dessert said to have been created by M. Mouy, chef to the Russian Count Nesselrode. It is chestnut purèe mixed with custard made of egg yolks, sugar, and cream or milk; or in place of the custard, ice cream flavored with Maraschino and mixed with whipped cream studded with candied orange peel, chopped cherries, currants, and raisins steeped in sweet wine or perhaps brandy. This is chilled in a mold and served, classically, ringed with a garnish of glazed chestnuts. This pudding is sometimes used as a pie filling in NESSELRODE PIE. Chopped nuts, especially almonds, are sometimes added, and it may be topped with shaved chocolate.

NEW ENGLAND STYLE A style of clam chowder (CHOW-du) made with milk as opposed to tomato, as in Manhattan-style clam chowder.

NEWBURG, LOBSTER A casserole of chunks of lobster, said to have been invented at New York City's Delmonico's restaurant. The chunks of lobster meat are sautéed in butter and served in a sauce made with cream, egg yolks, Sherry (brandy is sometimes substituted), and a sprinkling of paprika, or occasionally hot pepper.

NIÇOISE (nee-SWAHZ) *Fr.* Dishes described as done in the style of Nice generally feature seafood and vegetables, and the two most frequently used ingredients are tomatoes and garlic. Olive oil, anchovies, and ripe olives are also frequently encountered in these recipes.

SALADE NIÇOISE (sa-LAD) The salad of Nice is made up of quartered tomatoes, black olives, green peppers, raw broad beans, radishes, often fillets of anchovies and hard-boiled eggs, frequently greens and tuna (although not in the classic recipe), perhaps capers, and dressed with a vinaigrette dressing of oil and vinegar seasoned with garlic. Cooked green beans and diced potatoes are often included also, but apparently never in Nice.

NID, AU (oh nih) *Fr.* In a nest. The type of nests found in restaurants are generally nests of deep-fried potato straws. What we find in these nests is usually poultry (a bird in the nest rather than, say, beef in the nest, which would seem a bit peculiar). The nests are often lined with a crêpe to hold in the sauce which the tidbits are served in.

NIVERNAISE, À LA (nee-ver-NAEZ) *Fr.* In the style of Nevers. A garnish for meats, of carrots cut in small oval shapes and small glazed onions.

NOCE (NOH-chae) *It.* Nuts, especially walnuts.

NOISETTE, BEURRE (buhr nwah-ZET) *Fr.* Butter heated till it turns the brown color of a hazelnut, or filbert.

NOISETTES (nwah-ZET) *Fr.* Nuts, hazelnuts specifically. But also a cut of meat, often lamb—a small, thick, round, boneless slice from a tender cut, often loin.

74

NOIX (nwah) *Fr.* Nuts, specifically walnuts. When speaking of meat, though, this is a roast, usually rump or round.

NORMANDE, À LA (nawr-MAHₙD) *Fr.* In the style of Normandy, a region famous for its dairy products and its apples—its cider and its Calvados. Also its seafood. And these are the ingredients to expect in a dish described as à la Normande—not necessarily all together, but one or a few of them. Meat in the Norman style is often cooked in cider laced with Calvados. Poultry is often prepared the same way, and/or with cream and apples. Veal may be prepared in a cream sauce with mushrooms. In fish dishes à la Normande will often mean the fish is poached in white wine and served in a SAUCE NORMANDE (sohs), a cream sauce made with butter, flour, fish broth, cream, egg yolk, and perhaps bits of mushrooms, and served garnished with mussels, oysters, often mushrooms if not in the sauce, and perhaps shrimp or even crayfish.

MATELOTE À LA NORMANDE (ma-TLOHT) In Normandy Matelote is a saltwater fish stew, often prepared with cider, Calvados, butter, and cream.

NORVÉGIENNE, OMELETTE (awm-LET nawr-vae-ZHYEN) *Fr.* This "Norwegian omelette" is none other than our Baked Alaska—a slice of ice cream on a slice of sponge cake, generally sprinkled with liqueur, encased in meringue (egg whites whipped with sugar), and browned in the oven. It may even be flamed.

NOUILLE (nooy) *Fr.* Egg noodles.

O (oh) *It.* Or.
OCA (OH-kah) *It.* Goose.

OEUF, OEUFS (uhf, uh) *Fr.* Egg, eggs.

OIE (wah) *Fr.* Goose.

OIGNON (aw-NYAWn) *Fr.* Onion.

SOUPE À L'OIGNON (soop al) French onion soup, made with thinly sliced onions browned in butter, cooked in water or broth, sometimes wine, often thickened with a little flour, and lightly seasoned. When the soup is served au Gratin, GRATINÉE (gra-tee-NAE), a slice of toast topped with grated cheese browned to a crust is floated on top of the soup.

OISEAUX SANS TÊTE (wah-ZOH sahn taet) *Bl.* Literally, birds without heads, but this dish really isn't birds at all—it's thin slices of meat, usually beef, but sometimes veal, pounded flat and rolled around a stuffing of meat—bacon, ground pork or veal, or sausage meat—and perhaps bread crumbs and egg and seasonings, browned in butter with onions and sometimes mushrooms, celery, or green pepper, and cooked in broth, or perhaps beer, as is traditional in Belgium.

OLIO, ALL' (OH-lyoh) *It.* Prepared with oil, olive oil, OLIO DI OLIVA (dee oh-LEE-vah).

ORANGE, À L' (aw-RAHnZH) *Fr.* A style of preparing duck, CANARD (ka-NAR), or duckling, CANETON (kan-TAWn). The bird is roasted and served with a sauce of duck juices and white wine with a little sugar, vinegar, and butter, a splash of Port and a dash of Curaçao or other orange-based liqueur, thickened with a little cornstarch and seasoned with chopped parsley, sage, and bay leaf, and thin strips of orange peel; served garnished with orange sections.

OREGANATA (oh-rae-gah-NAH-tah) *It.* Prepared with oregano; frequently clams, VONGOLE (VOHN-goh-lae), sprinkled with chopped oregano, oil, and often bread crumbs, and baked in their shells.

ORIENTALE (aw-ryahn-TAL) *Fr.* Dishes described as Eastern or Oriental are usually garnished with tomatoes stuffed with saffron rice, or with rice pilaff, and tomato sauce.

ORLOFF, PRINCE ORLOFF, *Fr.* A style of preparing veal, VEAU (voh), created for the Russian prince by his chef. The veal is roasted, sliced, and stuffed between the slices with a mixture of puréed rice and onions and chopped mushrooms cooked in butter, sometimes grated Parmesan or Gruyère cheese, and a little cream, combined with a sauce of butter, flour, veal broth, cream, and a touch of nutmeg. Some of the sauce is spread over the whole roast, which is dusted with grated cheese and browned in the oven; sometimes made without the crust of cheese.

ORLY, À L' (ohr-LEE) *Fr.* A style of preparing fish, usually fish fillets, which are dipped in a light batter and deep fried. Accompanied with tomato sauce on the side. Frequently garnished with sprigs of parsley, sometimes fried parsley.

OSEILLE (oh-ZAEY) *Fr.* Sorrel, a slightly sour herb.

OSSI BUCHI, OSSOBUCO (OH-see BOO-kee, oh-soh-BOO-koh) *It.* A specialty of Milan—braised veal shanks, floured, browned in butter, and cooked in white wine with tomatoes. In the Milanese style, it is sprinkled with chopped parsley, garlic, mashed anchovies, and grated lemon rind. Some people feel the best part of this dish is the marrow in these "bone holes." Sometimes a special narrow spoon is served to scoop out the marrow. Ossobuco is traditionally served with Risotto alla Milanese, which see, under Milanese.

OSTRICHE (oh-STREE-kae) *It.* Sorry to disappoint

those of you who may have been feeling gastronomically adventurous, but it's not the big bird—only oysters.

OU (oo) *Fr.* Or.

PAELLA (pah-AE-yah) *Sp.* The classic rice dish of Spain, named for the large, shallow, two-handled pan in which the dish is cooked, and often served. This is rice cooked in broth and seasoned with saffron (which gives it its golden color), garlic, onions, often tomatoes, pimientos, sweet red peppers, sometimes olives, and vegetables such as green beans, kidney beans, peas, and perhaps artichoke hearts, and a variety of meats, chicken, sausage, and/or fish and shellfish. The particular mix is determined by the season, the region, and the discretion of the chef.

PAELLA VALENCIANA (bah-laen-thee-AH-nah) In the Paella of Valencia, the saffron rice is studded with green peas, string beans, sometimes kidney beans and artichoke hearts; and topped with chunks of chicken, often sausages, sometimes pork, ham, or veal, occasionally beef, and pieces of fish, and shellfish—clams and/or mussels, shrimp, sometimes eel and scallops, and maybe even lobster or crayfish, or squid.

PAGLIA E FIENO (PAH-lyah ae FYAE-noh) *It.* Literally, straw and hay. This is yellow (egg) and green (spinach) noodles tossed together with one of a variety of different sauces, but peas and Prosciutto in a cream sauce is one of the most popular.

PAILLARD (pa-YAR) A thin steak of veal or beef, usually grilled. Named after the Paris restaurateur who created, or popularized, it.

PALMIER, COEUR DE (kuhr duh pal-MYAE) *Fr.* Hearts of palm.

PALOMBE (pa-lawnb) *Fr.* Pigeon, squab.

PALOURDES (pa-LOORD) *Fr.* Clams.

PAMPLEMOUSSE (pan-plu-MOOS) *Fr.* Grapefruit.

PANACHÉ (pa-na-SHAE) *Fr.* Mixed.

PANÉ (pa-NAE) *Fr.* Breaded, fried in crumbs.

PANNA (PAHN-nah) *It.* Cream.

PANNA MONTATA (mohn-TAH-tah) Whipped cream.

PANNEQUETS (pan-KAE) *Fr.* Pancakes French style; that is, Crêpes, which see.

PANETTONE (pah-naet-TOH-nae) *It.* The tall golden coffee cake of Milan. It is made with yeast, flour, a little milk or water, not a lot of sugar, but plenty of butter and egg yolks, and flavored with grated lemon peel and vanilla and studded with light and dark raisins and candied citron.

PAPILLOTE, EN (ahn pa-pee-YAWT) *Fr.* In cooking paper. Food prepared in this fashion is baked in its own juices in a pocket of buttered, greaseproof paper. The paper holds in the aromas, which are released when the diner opens the little package in his dish.

PARFAIT (par-FAE) *Fr.* This "perfect" confection can be one of two types of dessert. In America Parfait is a tall (parfait) glass filled in layers with fruit, often in syrup, ice cream, and whipped cream. In France, it is a frozen custard made with eggs, seasonings, and cream served in the tall glass to which it lends its name.

PARFAIT GLACÉ (gla-SAE) Ice cream.

PARISIENNE, À LA (pa-ree-ZYEN) *Fr.* Dishes in the style of Paris will generally be served with a vegetable garnish including POMMES DE TERRE À LA PARISIENNE (pawm duh taer), which are little balls of potato about the size of an acorn, sautéed in butter, glazed with meat gravy, and sprinkled with chopped parsley.

PARMENTIER (par-mahn-TYAE) *Fr.* Dishes called

Parmentier will invariably include potatoes in one form or another in their makeup. Antoine-Auguste Parmentier, a French agronomist, was the single person most responsible for winning acceptance among the French for the lowly potato, as it was considered then, in the late eighteenth century.

POTAGE PARMENTIER (paw-TAHZH) Purée of potato soup flavored with sliced leeks cooked in butter, and enriched with cream or extra butter; served sprinkled with chopped chives, parsley, or chervil.

PARMIGIANA, ALLA (pahr-mee-JAH-nah) *It.* This may mean that the dish is prepared as they do in Parma, or more likely, that it is prepared with the famous cheese of Parma—Parmigiano (Parmesan), in which case it may be a recipe from a different region of Italy entirely, such as Naples, where they use tomato sauce and their own Mozzarella cheese, as well as Parmigiano, in these dishes.

ASPARAGI ALLA PARMIGIANA (ah-SPAH-rah-jee) Asparagus, like a number of other vegetables, as prepared in Parma are boiled and cooked in butter with grated Parmigiano (Parmesan) cheese.

MELANZANE ALLA PARMIGIANA (mae-lahn-DZAH-nae) This is eggplant prepared Parma or Naples style. The Neapolitan way fries thinly sliced eggplant in olive oil, then bakes it in a casserole with tomato sauce seasoned with basil, slices of Mozzarella cheese, and sometimes egg, topped with grated Parmesan cheese. In Parma, though, they make this dish with thin slices of Parma ham (Prosciutto) and without the Mozzarella.

POLLO ALLA PARMIGIANA (POHL-loh) Slices of chicken dipped in egg and bread crumbs, sautéed in butter, and topped with tomato sauce and slices of Mozzarella cheese. Parma style may use another soft, melting cheese.

SCALOPPINE DI VITELLO ALLA PARMIGIANA (skah-lohp-PEE-nae dee vee-TAEL-loh) Veal cutlets in this style are prepared the same way as the chicken, Pollo alla Parmigiana—or is it the other way around?

PASTA (PAH-stah) *It.* Pasta is the product of a flour and water, flour and egg, or flour, egg, and spinach paste which is dried, then boiled, then sometimes also baked with a sauce or filling. The flour and water pastas—Macaroni, Spaghetti, etc.—are usually not homemade anymore. The egg pastas, or noodles—Fettucine, Tortellini, etc.—are homemade, ALLA CASALINGA (kah-zah-LEEN-gah), in the better restaurants. The shapes are seemingly endless and evidence quite a lively imagination, as do many of the names.

PASTA E FAGIOLI, PASTA FAZOOL See Fagioli, Pasta e

PASTICCERIA (pah-stee-chae-REE-ah) *It.* Pastry.

PASTICCIO (pah-STEE-choh) *It.* Pie; also Paté, which see.

PATATA (pah-TAH-tah) *It.* Potato.

PATATE (pa-TAT) *Fr.* Sweet potato.

PÂTÉ (pah-TAE) *Fr.* Pâtés are rich loaves of ground meat, poultry, liver, or game mixed together with pork fat, distinctively seasoned, and often spiked with a little brandy or Port or Madeira. They are baked and (usually) cooled, and served sliced, often with a garnish of lettuce, gherkins, and perhaps a sprig of parsley, and sometimes chopped aspic. A Paté, such as house Paté, PÂTÉ MAISON (mae-ZAWn), not named for its basic ingredient, will frequently be made with chicken liver in this country, pork and veal in France. (It wouldn't hurt to ask your waiter on this one.) Patés were originally baked in a pastry ("pâté") crust, but the name has been adopted for the same type of meat loaf baked encased in strips of pork fat, without the crust to which it owes its name. Paté in a crust is often designated EN CROÛTE (ahn kroot). Patés may be silky smooth, rough and chunky, or somewhere in between. They may incorporate pieces of ham, veal, poultry, liver, or other meat, hard-boiled eggs, pistachio nuts, or even truffles. Truffled Patés are usually billed as such, PÂTÉ DE ... TRUFFÉE (trew-FAE).

PÂTÉ DE CAMPAGNE (duh kam-PA-nyu) Country-style Paté tends to be chunky, coarser in texture than its urban counterpart.

PÂTÉ CHAUD (shoh) Hot Paté maintains the classical tradition; that is, it is baked in a pastry crust. Hot Patés may be filled with any of the Paté mixtures. Gravy or an appropriate sauce is sometimes ladled over Pâté Chaud.

PÂTISSERIES (pa-tee-SREE) *Fr.* Pastries.

PAUPIETTES (poh-PYET) *Fr.* Thin slices of meat—if veal, they are what we call veal birds—spread with ground meat mixed with egg white and seasonings or similar stuffing, rolled up, sometimes wrapped in bacon, especially for beef, and braised in a small amount of wine or other liquid, sometimes with chopped onions cooked in butter. Fish, often sole, DE SOLES (duh sohl), may also be prepared in this style. The fish fillets are spread with fish pounded with seasonings and egg white or other stuffing, rolled up, and cooked in fish broth or sauce, or simply in butter.

PAVESE, ZUPPA ALLA (DZOOP-pah pah-VAE-zae) *It.* The famous soup of Pavia. Classically made, slices of bread sautéed in butter are dusted with grated Parmesan cheese, then placed in the soup bowl and topped with a raw egg, or just the yolk. Then boiling consommé is poured over it, which poaches the egg. Often, though, the egg is poached before being placed on the toast as this gives an egg which is more thoroughly cooked, and doesn't run the risk of disconcerting squeamish diners. Extra cheese accompanies the soup. According to the story, the dish was invented by a peasant of Pavia in Lombardy for François I of France, who was fighting a losing battle against the Spanish there in 1525. Called upon to provide a meal for the king, the peasant (in some versions, a young signorina) rose to the occasion with this soup made with the usual stock-pot broth but enriched for the royal palate.

PAYSANNE, À LA (pae-ee-ZAHN) *Fr.* A preparation for meat or poultry, peasant style—which usually means braised and served with sliced or coarsely chopped root vegetables such as onions, turnips, carrots, and celery cooked in butter, sometimes also pieces of bacon or salt pork.

PÊCHES (paesh) *Fr.* Peaches.

PEPE (pae-pae) *It.* Pepper.

PEPERONATA (pae-pae-roh-NAH-tah) *It.* A dish of peppers, red and green, cut in strips and cooked with sliced onions in oil and butter, and chopped tomatoes, spiced with garlic, bay leaf, and pepper. Other vegetables such as celery, or carrot, are sometimes added. May be served hot or cold.

PEPERONCINI (pae-pae-rohn-CHEE-nee) *It.* Hot chili peppers, fresh or dried.

PEPERONI (pae-pae-ROH-nee) *It.* Sweet peppers, green or red (pimientos). In the U.S.A. this name is given also to a spicy—peppery—hard sausage.

PEPERONI E ACCIUGHE (ae ah-CHOO-gae)

83

Wide slices of sweet pepper, roasted and curled around anchovy fillets. Often sprinkled with capers and marinated in oil and wine vinegar or lemon juice and seasoned with oregano and/or parsley.

PERDREAU, PERDRIX (paer-DROH, paer-DREE) *Fr.* Partridge.

PERE (PAE-rae) *It.* Pears.

PÉRIGEUX, SAUCE (sohs pae-ree-GUH) *Fr.* The sauce of the Périgord is made of rich meat broth flavored with Madeira and truffle essence, and sprinkled with chopped truffles—those truffles for which this region is famous.

PÉRIGOURDINE, À LA (pae-ree-goor-DEEN) *Fr.* In the style of the Périgord, a region famous for its truffles. Dishes prepared in this style are sure to contain truffles, and often the other specialty of the region as well—foie gras. Often these goodies are contained in the sauce served with the dish.

FILET DE BOEUF EN CROÛTE PÉRIGOURDINE (fee-LAE duh BUHF ahn KROOT) Roast fillet or tenderloin of beef spread with pâté de foie gras, or sometimes a mixture of sautéed chopped mushrooms and perhaps shallots, seasoned with Madeira and combined with foie gras, wrapped in a pastry crust (en Croûte), and baked. It is served with Sauce Périgourdine.

SAUCE PÉRIGOURDINE (sohs) Virtually the same as Sauce Périgeux; under this name, a purée of goose liver is sometimes added to the sauce.

PERNICE (paer-NEE-chae) *It.* Partridge.

PERSILLADE (paer-see-YAD) *Fr.* Chopped parsley, often mixed with chopped garlic; sprinkled over roast meats, etc.

PERSILLÉ (paer-see-YAE) *Fr.* Sprinkled with chopped parsley.

POMMES DE TERRE PERSILLÉES (pawm duh

taer) Parslied potatoes, which are boiled, rolled in melted butter, and sprinkled with chopped parsley.

CARRÉ or GIGOT D'AGNEAU (ka-RAE, zhih-GOH da-NYOH) Roast rack, or leg, of lamb coated with chopped parsley; often combined with chopped garlic and/or bread crumbs.

PESCE (PAE-shae) *It.* Fish.

PESCE SPADA (SPAH-dah) Swordfish.

PESCHE (PAE-skae) *It.* Peaches.

PESTO (PE-stoh) *It.* The basil sauce of Liguria. Fresh basil is crushed and mixed—in your trusty mortar and pestle, traditionally (the word means "pounded")—with garlic, Parmesan cheese (sometimes mixed with the stronger Pecorino, especially in Italy), olive oil (sometimes with butter), and pine nuts (walnuts are sometimes substituted).

PETITS-FOURS (pu-TEE FOOR) *Fr.* Literally, little things from the oven. These are fancy, bite-sized cakes, decoratively frosted and embellished; also certain types of cookies, such as macaroons.

PÉTONCLES (pae-TAWnKL) *Fr.* Scallops.

PIACERE, A (ah pyah-CHAE-rae) *It.* Prepared "to (your) pleasure," in the style you wish.

PIATTO (PYAHT-toh) *It.* Plate.

PIATTO DEL GIORNO (dael JOHR-noh) Dish of the day, daily specialty.

PIATTO FREDDO (FRAED-doh) Cold plate, plate of cold delicacies.

PICCANTE (peek-KAHN-tae) *It.* Piquant, spicy.

PICCATA (peek-KAH-tah) *It.* A style of preparing veal cutlets, SCALOPPINE (skah-lohp-PEE-nae), which are sautéed in butter and sprinkled with lemon juice.

PICCIONE (pee-CHOH-nae) *It.* Pigeon.

PIEDS (pye) *Fr.* Feet. The most usual feet on the menu are pig's trotters, DE COCHON or DE

PORC (duh kaw-SHAWₙ, pawr), but sometimes you will also see sheep's trotters, DE MOUTON (moo-TAWₙ).

PIEMONTESE, ALLA (pyae-mohn-TAE-zae) *It.* In the style of Piemonte (Piedmont), a region famous for its rice and its truffles—white ones. Fontina cheese, garlic, and anchovies are also frequently used in the cooking of the Piedmont.

GNOCCHI ALLA PIEMONTESE (NYOHK-kee) Here, these little dumplings are often made with potatoes, as well as flour and eggs.

RISOTTO ALLA PIEMONTESE (ree-ZOHT-toh) This is rice cooked in butter and meat broth; pieces of salt pork and/or Prosciutto are sometimes included; lots of grated Parmesan cheese is stirred in; and, of course, the famous white truffles of Piedmont, sliced paper thin.

PIGEON, PIGEONNEAU (pee-ZHAWₙ, pee-zhawn-NOH) *Fr.* Squab, pigeon.

PIGNOLI (pee-NYOH-lee) *It.* Pine nuts.

PILAF, PILAU (PEE-lahf, pee-LAHF) *Trk.* A Turkish rice dish. The rice is cooked in butter or oil, then boiled in broth or water seasoned with herbs and spices. Pilaf may be served plain, but very often other ingredients are mixed in—meat, poultry, fish, pine nuts, chick-peas, onions, mushrooms, pasta, currants—whatever the cook deems complementary.

PIMIENTO (pee-MYAEN-toh) Sweet red peppers, often marinated.

PINTADE (pan-TAD) *Fr.* Guinea hen.

PIPÉRADE (pee-pe-RAD) *Fr.* A specialty of the Basque region. This is chopped onions and sweet red peppers sautéed in oil, mixed with coarsely chopped tomatoes and seasonings such as garlic and basil, mixed together with eggs into sort of a scrambled omelette. Pipérade is served with a garnish of grilled ham or bacon—over there, it would be the local Bayonne ham.

PISELLI, PISELLINI (pee-ZAEL-lee, pee-zael-LEE-nee) *It.* Green peas, tiny green peas.

PISTACHE, EN (ahn pees-TASH) *Fr.* A style of cooking from the Pyrenées, which has nothing to do with pistachio nuts; no sir—garlic cloves, and lots of them, are what these dishes are cooked with.

PISTACHES, AUX (oh pees-TASH) *Fr.* With pistachio nuts—not to be confused with En Pistache, above.

PISTOU, SOUPE AU (soop oh pees-TOO) *Fr.* A Provençal soup of mixed vegetables, and often pasta such as vermicelli, seasoned with fresh chopped basil and garlic, olive oil, and often grated Parmesan cheese. Does it sound more Italian than French? Well, you could call it Minestrone al Genovese and it would come out to the same thing.

PIZZAIOLA, ALLA (pee-tsah-YOH-lah) *It.* A Neapolitan sauce made with tomatoes, olive oil, garlic, sometimes green peppers, and/or chopped onions, seasoned with oregano, black pepper, and sometimes basil and bay leaf. You may even encounter a mushroom or two; this seems to be a sauce that invites interpretation and variation.

POCHÉ (paw-SHAE) *Fr.* Poached.

POÊLE, À LA or POÊLÉE (pwahl, pwah-LAE) *Fr.* Cooked in a frying pan; pan-fried.

POIREAUX (pwah-ROH) *Fr.* Leeks.

POIRES (pwahr) *Fr.* Pears.

POIRES AU VIN (zoh van) Whole peeled pears poached, or baked, in wine—usually red wine, which dyes the pears a rosy red. The wine is sweetened with sugar, sometimes thinned with water, and may be flavored with lemon juice, cinnamon, or cloves. Served cold.

POIS, PETIT POIS (pwah, pu-TEE) *Fr.* Green peas, tiny green peas.

POISSON (pwah-SAWn) *Fr.* Fish.

POITRINE DE (pwah-TREEN duh) *Fr.* Breast of.

POIVRADE (pwahv-RAD) *Fr.* A peppery sauce of onions, celery, carrot, and shallots sautéed in butter, thickened with a little flour, and cooked in white wine and meat broth seasoned with a little wine vinegar, thyme, bay leaf, perhaps cloves, and, of course, a generous sprinkling of cracked peppercorns.

POIVRE (pwahvr) *Fr.* Pepper.

STEAK AU POIVRE Generally sirloin or porterhouse steak, coated with coarsely ground peppercorns which are pressed into the meat on both sides; the steak is, traditionally, sautéed in oil and/or butter, but it may be broiled. Sometimes flamed with cognac. Sometimes it is served with a cream sauce made with heavy or sour cream and Cognac and perhaps onions cooked in butter, a touch of tomato, parsley, thyme and bay leaf, white wine and Port. Then, again, it may be served in a sauce of butter, shallots or scallions, white wine or vermouth, and beef broth; flamed with Cognac or not, depending on the restaurant's sense of drama.

POLENTA (poh-LAEN-tah) *It.* A cornmeal specialty of northern Italy. The cornmeal is boiled, and served with butter, cheese, pan juices, or tomato or meat sauce—or a combination of any of the preceding. Polenta may also be cooled, then fried or baked before the toppings go on, or even reheated with them.

POLLO (POHL-loh) *It.* Chicken.

PETTI DI POLLO (PAET-tee dee) Breast of chicken.

POLONAISE, À LA (paw-law-NAEZ) *Fr.* Polish style, as interpreted by the French. In this style, the particular food, often cauliflower, CHOU-FLEUR (shoo-FLUHR), or asparagus, ASPERGE (as-PAERZH), is topped with bread crumbs browned in butter and chopped hard-boiled eggs, or just the yolks, and parsley.

POLPETTE, POLPETTINE (pohl-PAET-tae, pohl-paet-TEE-nae) *It.* This usually means meatballs, often floured before being sautéed. They may be made from raw or cooked meat, are sometimes made from fish, occasionally vegetables, but this should be indicated in the name; the non-meat versions would be Croquettes.

POLPETTONE (pohl-paet-TOH-nae) *It.* Meatloaf or roll, sometimes of fish or vegetables. Like Polpette, this term is equivalent to Croquette (a big croquette), so—meat, poultry, fish, or vegetables may be used. But if the name doesn't specify, you can expect to get meatloaf.

POLPO (POHL-poh) *It.* Octopus.

POMME (pawm) *Fr.* Apple.

POMME DE TERRE (pawm duh taer) *Fr.* "Earth apple," or more prosaically, potato.

POMME DE TERRE EN ROBE DE CHAMBRE (ahn rawb duh shanbr) "Potato in its dressing gown," or as we would say, its jacket, which for potatoes are their skins—which they are baked in.

POMMES (DE TERRE) FRITES (pawm freet) Deep-fried potatoes, or as we (but not they) would say, French fried potatoes.

POMIDORO, POMODORO (poh-mee-DOH-roh, poh-moh-DOH-roh) *It.* Tomato; literally, "golden apple" (it is believed that the first tomatoes imported into Europe from South America in the sixteenth century were yellow).

AL POMODORO With tomato sauce, generally a fairly simple sauce of tomatoes, olive oil, sometimes chopped onion, and/or garlic, perhaps white wine, and seasoned with parsley or basil.

POMPELMO (pohm-PAEL-moh) *It.* Grapefruit.

PORC (pawr) *Fr.* Pork.

PORCELET (pawr-su-LAE) *Fr.* Suckling pig.

PORCHETTA (pohr-KAET-tah) *It.* Roast suckling pig, often seasoned with rosemary.

PORCO (POHR-koh) *It.* Pork.

PORTO, AU (oh pawr-TOH) *Fr.* With Port sauce, a rich sauce of concentrated meat broth flavored with spices and Port wine.

PORTUGAISE, À LA (pawr-tew-GAEZ) *Fr.* Prepared or garnished with tomatoes, often seasoned with garlic and onion. Or cooked with Portuguese sauce.

SAUCE PORTUGAISE (sohs) Made with tomatoes, olive oil, garlic, onion, meat broth or wine, and chopped parsley.

POSILLIPO (poh-SEEL-lee-poh) *It.* Preparation for shellfish, usually mussels, COZZE (KOH-tsae), or clams, VONGOLE (VOHN-goh-lae), steamed and served in a sauce of tomato, olive oil, garlic, and parsley; in the style of Cape Posillipo in the Bay of Naples.

POTAGE (paw-TAHZH) *Fr.* Soup.

POT-AU-FEU (paw-toh-FUH) *Fr.* Literally, the pot on the fire. This was the pot always kept hot on the back of the farmhouse stove in the days of woodstoves. In those days they just kept adding—meat and seasonal vegetables to replace what was ladled out for dinner. Today, there is a basic recipe, subject to regional variation. This is beef, sometimes with veal, sometimes with chicken, or simply with beef bones, stewed with vegetables, usually

90

leeks, onions, carrots, often turnips and cabbage, and sometimes celery, seasoned with bay leaf, thyme, parsley, often peppercorns, garlic, and cloves. Pot-au-Feu provides a two-course dinner. Traditionally, the clear broth is served first (soup course) often floating slices of toast; then the meat is served on a platter surrounded with the vegetables (main dish).

POTTED *Br.* Conserved in a pot, as Potted Crab, Potted Char (a type of fish), etc. This is meat, poultry, fish, or game cooked in a broth with seasonings, sealed with melted butter in a pot, and cooled.

POTÉE (paw-TAE) *Fr.* Literally, a potful. This is a potful of stew, traditionally in an earthenware pot, made usually with pork and vegetables, mostly cabbage and potatoes, though the ingredients are variable and may include other meats as well as vegetables such as kidney beans.

POULARDE (poo-LARD) *Fr.* Chicken, roaster.

POULE (pool) *Fr.* Hen.

POULE AU POT (oh poh) This is your original "chicken in the pot," named by King Henri IV of France as the Sunday dinner he wanted all of his subjects to enjoy. The hen is stuffed with the chicken liver, bread crumbs, and egg, sometimes chopped fresh pork or sausage meat, or even better and perhaps more reflective of the original—Bayonne ham (from Henri's home region), and flavored with garlic, perhaps onion, parsley, and sometimes nutmeg, and a splash of Armagnac. It is simmered in a rich broth, then served with the broth or with a cream sauce using the broth as a base. This dish is sometimes described as POULE AU POT À LA BÉARNAISE (be-ar-NAEZ), after Henri IV, who was from Béarn.

POULET (poo-LAE) *Fr.* Chicken, broiler.

POULET DE GRAIN (duh gran) Corn-fed chicken.

POULETTE (poo-LET) *Fr.* A sauce made of chicken or veal broth, egg yolk, thickened with flour and butter, and flavored with mushrooms, lemon juice, and chopped parsley.

POUSSIN (poo-SAn) *Fr.* Spring chicken, squab chicken.

PRALIN, AU or PRALINÉ (oh pra-LAn, pra-lee-NAE) *Fr.* Flavored with burnt sugar and vanilla mixed with ground toasted almonds.

PRAWNS   Large shrimp (about 3 to 4 inches long).

PRESSE, À LA (pres) *Fr.* Pressed, as in Pressed Duck, CANARD (ka-NAR), or CANETON (kan-TAWn). The duck is roasted, then carved and served with a sauce made from red wine, a little brandy, and the juices from the pieces of the duck which have been put into a duck press—at your table—where the duck essence is pressed out. The sauce is heated with a little butter and poured over the meat.

PRESSED DUCK   See Presse, à la above.

PREZZEMOLO (pret-TSAE-moh-loh) *It.* Parsley.

PRIMEURS, AUX (oh pree-MUHR) *Fr.* Served with early vegetables, the first of the season.

PRINCESSE, À LA (pran-SES) *Fr.* Dishes prepared in the style of the princess are garnished with asparagus tips in butter or cream and truffles, sliced or diced.

PRINTANIÈRE, À LA (pran-ta-NYAER) *Fr.* These "springlike" dishes are garnished with early carrots and turnips and string beans cut to uniform size, new green peas and asparagus tips cooked in butter.

POTAGE PRINTANIÈRE (paw-TAHZH) Vegetable soup made with the early vegetables of the season.

PRIX FIXE, À (pree feeks) *Fr.* At a fixed price.

PROFITEROLES (praw-fee-te-RAWL) *Fr.* Balls of puff pastry about the size of a walnut filled with whipped cream, custard cream, or even ice cream and topped with a sweet sauce, often chocolate sauce, or occasionally confectioners' sugar—like baby eclairs. Smaller Profiteroles may also be used, unsweetened, of course, and with a filling of cheese or the like, as a garnish in soups.

PROSCIUTTO (proh-SHOOT-toh) *It.* Ham. This usually refers to ham which has been cured by salting (but the best is not salty) and air-drying, rather than smoking.

PROVENÇALE, À LA (praw-vahn-SAL) *Fr.* In the style of Provence, where the cuisine is notable for its liberal use of garlic, and usually also tomatoes and olive oil, herbs and spices.

COQUILLES ST. JACQUES À LA PROVEN-ÇALE (kaw-KEEY san ZHAHK) Scallops floured and sautéed in oil and butter, and seasoned with garlic, shallots, lemon juice, and perhaps a little white wine. Sometimes garnished with chopped or broiled tomato.

GRENOUILLES À LA PROVENÇALE (gru-NUHY) Frogs' legs floured, sautéed in olive oil, sometimes with butter also, and seasoned with chopped parsley and garlic, and perhaps a dash of lemon juice.

PRUGNA (PROO-nyah) *It.* Plum.

PRUGNA SECCA (SAEK-kah) Prune, dried plum.

PRUNE (prewn) *Fr.* Plum.

PRUNEAU (prew-NOH) *Fr.* Prune.

PUTTANESCA, ALLA (poot-tah-NAES-kah) *It.* A

Neapolitan style of preparing Spaghetti. Literally, "as a prostitute would prepare it." Perhaps named for the apparently indiscriminate (promiscuous?) mixture of ingredients which go into the sauce: olive oil, garlic, tomatoes, capers, black olives, hot chili pepper, anchovies, chopped oregano and parsley, salt and black pepper.

QUAGLIE (KWAH-lyae) *It.* Quail.

QUENELLES (ku-NEL) *Fr.* Light, usually oval, dumplings of fish, poultry, or meat, Quenelles of pike, DE BROCHET (duh braw-SHAE), being the most popular. Quenelles are made with puréed fish (or meat) mixed with eggs, sometimes a little cream, and a paste of flour, butter, and water, often seasoned with a pinch of nutmeg. The dumplings are poached in salted water, which puffs them up to about twice their original size and gives them their airy texture, and served with a sauce—for Quenelles of pike, usually Nantua Sauce, which see.

QUEUE (kew) *Fr.* Tail. The tails you'll see in restaurants are usually one of two types: oxtail, QUEUE DE BOEUF (duh buhf), or rock lobster tails, QUEUE DE LANGOUSTE (lahn-GOOST).

QUICHE (keesh) *Fr.* A custard tart. The pastry crust is filled with a mixture of eggs and cream or, sometimes, milk and butter, to which a number of other goodies may be added—shellfish, cheese, mushrooms, spinach, ham or bacon, etc. It is often seasoned with nutmeg. Served hot or cold.

QUICHE LORRAINE (law-RAEN) Generally thought of as a Quiche with cheese, but the classic Quiche Lorraine doesn't contain any cheese. The pastry crust is filled with a mixture of eggs and cream poured over lightly fried bacon. This is often varied, though, by the addition of grated cheese, usually Gruyère, and/or the substitution of ham for the bacon. Some cooks even add onions, but this is really more of an Alsatian style of Quiche. Generally seasoned with nutmeg. Served hot or cold.

RACK The rack of lamb, or other meat, is a rib roast—several chops roasted together, then carved into chops.

RACLETTE (ra-KLET) *Sw.* A specialty of the Valais region of Switzerland. Traditionally made, a half-wheel (or what's left of it) of the local Bagnes, or Conches, cheese is held before an open fire and scraped as it melts onto a plate ("racler" means to scrape). This is garnished with little onions and perhaps gherkins. Potatoes boiled in their jackets accompany the dish.

RAFRAÎCHE, RAFRÎCHIS (ra-FRESH, ra-fre-SHEE) *Fr.* Fresh, cooled—refreshed by being cooled.

RAGOÛT (ra-GOO) *Fr.* Stew. Ragouts are made of meat, poultry, or fish, with or without vegetables, stewed in broth.

RAGÙ (rah-GOO) *It.* The rich meat sauce of Bologna, which is ladled over pasta. The Ragù sauce is made of chopped onions, celery, and carrot cooked in butter and oil, ground meat—beef and pork, perhaps veal, bacon, sometimes ham, sausage meat and/or chicken livers, stewed in white wine and broth, flavored with tomato paste and maybe a sprinkling of nutmeg. Some chefs add sliced sautéed mushrooms and many enrich the already rich sauce with cream. Grated Parmesan cheese gilds the sauce (and the lily).

RAIE (rae) *Fr.* Ray, skate fish.

RAIFORT (rae-FAWR) *Fr.* Horseradish sauce. This

sauce is made with cream or a blend of butter, flour, and milk, sparked with grated horseradish and a little vinegar or lemon juice.

RAISIN (rae-SAN) *Fr.* Grapes. Raisins, on the other hand, are RAISINS SECS (sek), dried grapes.

RANE (RAH-nae) *It.* Frogs, of which only the (back) legs, GAMBE DI RANE (GAHM-bae dee) are eaten.

RAREBIT (RABBIT) or WELSH RAREBIT (RABBIT), *Br.* A cheese dish of the British Isles. Nothing to do with furry creatures, this is grated Cheddar or similar cheese melted and mixed with beer or ale (milk for teetotalers), and sometimes butter and egg, often seasoned with mustard, and perhaps Worcestershire sauce. It is served poured over toast.

RATATOUILLE (ra-ta-TOOY) *Fr.* Diced eggplant, zucchini, tomatoes, green peppers (Provence and Nice often omit the peppers), and onions stewed in olive oil and seasoned with garlic, sometimes parsley, and perhaps even basil and thyme. This specialty of Provence is usually served cold, as an appetizer. As a side dish with meat or poultry, it may be served hot.

RAVIGOTE (ra-veeh-GAWT) *Fr.* Literally, a refresher, reviver. This generally refers to a cold sauce made with oil and vinegar (mayonnaise is sometimes used), capers, perhaps chopped hard-boiled eggs, and seasoned with minced onions, chives, chervil, parsley, tarragon, and, optionally, mustard. There is a less often encountered warm Ravigote Sauce (sohs) made with white wine, vinegar, shallots, cream, butter, flour, and spices similar to those in the cold version—parsley, chervil, chives, tarragon, thyme, and perhaps a little hot cayenne pepper. Many restaurants simplify the sauce, but there should still be enough herbs and spices for the sauce to be a refresher.

RAVIOLI (rah-VYOH-lee) *It.* The pasta of Genoa. Squares of pasta filled with a cheese or meat and/ or vegetable stuffing. Cheese Ravioli is generally filled with a mixture of Ricotta cheese, egg, grated Parmesan cheese, sometimes butter, perhaps a little grated onion and chopped parsley, and seasoned with nutmeg. Meat Ravioli, as a rule, is stuffed with a mixture of chopped onions cooked in butter and olive oil, sometimes also garlic, ground meat— veal or beef—egg, grated Parmesan cheese, perhaps bread crumbs, sometimes spinach, occasionally chopped tomato, and seasoned with a pinch of nutmeg, and sometimes chopped parsley. Ravioli may be served in broth, but usually is served with a tomato sauce or with butter and grated Parmesan cheese on top.

REGANATA (rae-gah-NAH-tah) *It.* Another way of saying Arreganata, which see.

REINE, À LA (raen) *Fr.* In the style of the queen. Dishes in the queenly style are generally made with chicken, puréed or cut up and served with mushrooms and truffles in a cream sauce.

CONSOMMÉ À LA REINE (kawn-saw-MAE) Chicken consommé thickened with tapioca and garnished with dices of Royale. This Royal Custard is made with eggs, cream, julienne strips of chicken and seasoned with chervil.

RÉMOULADE (rae-moo-LAD) *Fr.* A sauce of mayonnaise flavored with anchovy paste, mustard, chopped gherkins, capers, chervil, scallions, parsley, and sometimes tarragon. Some restaurants, though, offer a simpler version of the classic sauce.

RHUM, AU (oh rawm) *Fr.* With rum.

RICOTTA, TORTE or CROSTATA DI (TOHR-tah, kroh-STAH-tah, dee ree-KOHT-tah) *It.* Light cheese pie, sometimes called "Italian cheesecake." It is made with Ricotta cheese, eggs and sugar, flavored with cinnamon or vanilla, sometimes grated orange peel, candied citron or orange peel, raisins, and nuts such as almonds and pine nuts. The pastry crust may be flavored with lemon peel.

RIGATONI (ree-gah-TOH-nee) *It.* Groovy Macaroni—that is, short fat tubes of pasta with grooves, or furrows, which give the shape its name, Rigatoni—the big grooved ones.

RILLETTES (ree-YET) *Fr.* Pork cooked with pork fat in a little water and seasoned with salt, pepper, and spices such as garlic, sage, and bay leaf. It is shredded or pounded to a paste, put into a crock to cool, and sealed with a layer of pork fat. The city of Tours, DE TOURS (duh toowr), is famous for its Rillettes. The Rillettes of Le Mans, DE LE MANS (luh man), are made with goose as well as pork.

RIPIENE (ree-PYAE-nae) *It.* Stuffed.

RIS (ree) *Fr.* Sweetbread, which see. This may be either sweetbread of calf, DE VEAU (duh voh), or of lamb, D'AGNEAU (da-NYOH).

RISI E BISI (REE-zee ae BEE-zee) *It.* Rice and peas, a specialty of Venezia (Venice). This is generally listed on menus under "Soups," but if it's a soup, it must be the thickest one going; it is eaten with a fork. It is made with oil and butter, in which chopped celery, sometimes onion and garlic and even diced bacon are lightly browned. To this, bouillon and the rice are added and then the fresh green peas. Grated Parmesan cheese is sprinkled over the top.

RISO (REE-zoh) *It.* Rice.

RISOTTO (ree-ZOHT-toh) *It.* A rice dish of northern Italy. Rice lightly sautéed in butter, usually—but some regions use olive oil—with seasonings such as chopped onion, garlic, celery, carrot, etc., to which broth or wine or simply water is added, producing a creamy but still firm rice dish. Bits of meat, poultry, or fish and/or vegetables—tomatoes, asparagus tips, mushrooms, peas, fennel—and various seasonings (truffles, anchovies, parsley) are often added, although the simplest risotto is flavored with only butter, perhaps onion, and grated cheese. Parmesan cheese is virtually always grated into the Risotto. The few exceptions are fish and shellfish Risotto. Risotto often takes the place of pasta in the cooking of northern Italy.

RISSOLES (rih-SAWL) *Fr.* Ground meat in pastry. The meat, often cooked meat, is seasoned and wrapped in a pastry crust, then fried, often deep fried.

RIZ (ree) *Fr.* Rice.

ROBERT (roh-BAER) *Fr.* A piquant sauce made with onions cooked in butter, white wine, thick meat broth, flavored with a little tomato, parsley, thyme, and bay leaf; sometimes vinegar is added, and always mustard. The sauce is said to have been created by Robert Vinot in the early seventeenth century.

ROCKEFELLER, OYSTERS This dish was created late in the nineteenth century by Jules Alciatore, founder of Antoine's Restaurant in New Orleans, and believed to have gotten its name from the richness of the dish. The rendition varies from place to place, but basically this is oysters on the half shell baked topped with a purée of spinach, chopped green onions or shallots, celery, cooked in butter with chopped parsley, perhaps chervil or fennel, and bread crumbs, seasoned with a splash of Pernod or other aniseed-flavored liqueur, perhaps a dash of lime juice, and a touch of hot pepper.

ROGNONS (raw-NYAWn) *Fr.* Kidneys.

ROGNONCINI (roh-nyohn-CHEE-nee) *It.* Little

kidneys, that is, veal or lamb kidneys.

ROGNONI (roh-NYOH-nee) *It.* Kidneys.

ROLLATINE (rohl-lah-TEE-nae) *It.* Meat, usually veal or chicken breast, flattened with a cutlet bat and rolled up around a stuffing often containing Prosciutto, and cheese, and spices. These rolls, sometimes floured, are sautéed in (usually) butter and simmered in a little wine or broth, or perhaps in a particular sauce.

ROLLMOPS, ROLLMÖPSE (ROHL-mawps, ROHL-muhp-se) *Gm.* Herring fillets, marinated in a vinegar brine seasoned with spices such as mustard seed, black pepper, bay leaf, thyme, garlic, and sliced onions, rolled up around a gherkin or pickle.

ROMANA (roh-MAH-nah) *It.* In a salad, this means romaine lettuce. ALLA ROMANA means in the style of Rome, a city whose cooking is characterized by its use of mint and also Ricotta cheese.

CROSTINI ALLA ROMANA (kroh-STEE-nee) Pieces of toast and pieces of cheese, generally Mozzarella, threaded alternately on a skewer (or placed together without the skewers), baked in the oven, and spread with anchovy butter.

GNOCCHI ALLA ROMANA (NYOHK-kee) Dumplings of flour usually, but may be of potato, baked with lots of butter and grated Parmesan cheese.

LINGUINE ALLA ROMANA (leen-GWEE-nae) Thin ribbons of pasta ("little tongues") with a sauce of butter and Ricotta cheese.

SPIEDINI ALLA ROMANA (spyae-DEE-nee) The same dish as Crostini alla Romana, above, on skewers (spiedini).

ROMANOFF, ROMANOV (roh-ma-NAWF, roh-MAH-nawv) *Fr.* A style of serving fresh fruit, usually strawberries, FRAISES (fraez), which are steeped in orange juice and Curaçao or other orange-based liqueur and served with ice cream and/or whipped cream.

ROSETTE (roh-ZET) *Fr.* A large pork sausage which may get its name from the fact that its slices have a scalloped edge from the string that binds it. This sausage, a specialty of the Lyons district, is eaten uncooked, being cured, not fresh.

ROSMARINO (roh-zmah-REE-noh) *It.* Rosemary.

ROSSINI See Tournedos Rossini.

RÔTI (roh-TEE) *Fr.* Roasted, a roast (of meat).

ROUENNAISE, À LA (rwa-NAEZ) *Fr.* A Norman style of preparing duckling, CANARD (ka-NAR), or duck, CANETON (kan-TAWɴ), used especially for the Rouen duck, CANARD ROUENNAIS (rwa-NAE). This duck has a slightly gamey flavor due to the fact that it is nʊt bled when killed as are most ducks. Duck prepared in the style of Rouen in Normandy is roasted rare. The drumsticks are then grilled and the meat from the body carved into slices. This is served with SAUCE ROUENNAISE (sohs) made with shallots or onions cooked in butter, red wine, duck broth, sometimes the minced or pounded duck liver, chopped parsley, and the blood and juices of the parts of the duck sprinkled with lemon juice and brandy and pressed out in a duck press. Often the dish is flamed with brandy or Cognac.

ROULADE (roo-LAD) *Fr.* Rolled roast of meat or a thin slice of meat, usually of veal, DE VEAU (duh voh), or pork, PORC (pawr), spread with a filling, rolled up, and braised or poached like a Galantine.

ROULADEN (roo-LAH-den) *Gm.* This German specialty is slices of beef, RINDSROULADEN (RIHNTS-roo-lah-den) rolled up around a stuffing, perhaps of chopped meat, often of bacon and/or a gherkin, and browned in fat, sometimes with chopped onion, then simmered in liquid such as bouillon or wine.

ROYALE (rwah-YAL) *Fr.* A custard garnish for clear soups made with eggs and cream or broth, and sometimes a vegetable or meat purée. It is cut into decorative shapes and floated in the soup. There is also a SAUCE ROYALE (sohs) used especially for poultry which has been poached. The sauce is made with flour and butter, perhaps egg yolk, chicken broth, cream, a touch of Sherry, and perhaps bits of truffles. Other dishes described as Royale are prepared in a rich or regal style as interpreted by the chef.

RUGOLA (ROO-goh-lah) *It.* An aromatic salad green which resembles (in appearance—not taste) cultivated dandelion. Called rocket or rockette in English.

RUSSE, À LA (roos) *Fr.* Dishes prepared in the Russian style, as interpreted by the French, tend to have either sour cream or caviar in their makeup. Or they may be made with SAUCE RUSSE (sohs), a base of mayonnaise to which are added purée of caviar and lobster coral with mustard, such as OEUFS À LA (uh za la) RUSSE—hard-boiled eggs topped with this sauce.

SALADE À LA RUSSE (sa-LAD) Sort of a Russian chef's salad of diced, or julienne, vegetables such as cucumbers, carrots, celery, onion or green onion, perhaps turnip, sometimes lettuce, cooked or raw mushrooms, cooked potatoes, beets, green beans, and peas, with cooked meats also in cubes or in strips—ham, tongue, salami, chicken, pork (some or all of these)—and often chunks of lobster or crayfish. The salad is dressed with mayonnaise, and traditionally formed into a dome shape. It is garnished with tidbits like anchovy fillets, hard-boiled eggs, pickles, capers, sometimes truffles, tomato quarters, green or black olives, or pimientos.

SABAYON (sa-ba-YAWn) *Fr.* The French version of the Italian Zabaglione. This pudding is made with egg yolks, sugar, and white wine, and flavored with vanilla or other seasoning such as lemon or orange peel or liqueurs, not necessarily Marsala, as in Zabaglione. Sabayon is often garnished with fruit, or served as a sauce over fruit such as strawberries, FRAISES (fraez).

SADDLE A roast of meat comprising both loins and often the kidneys as well. A single serving, needless to say, will be only a cut from the saddle, not the whole thing.

SAINTE-MENEHOULD (sant-mae-nae-OOL) *Fr.* A method of preparing bony cuts of meat such as pig's or sheep's feet, breast of veal or lamb, or oxtail—originally pig's feet, presumably, as Ste.-Menehould is a district famous for its pork products, especially pig's feet. In this style, the meat is first simmered in water seasoned with onion, carrots, parsley, celery, bay leaf, thyme, and sometimes bits of bacon. It is then boned and coated with butter and breadcrumbs, sometimes with egg, and in some cases seasoned with mustard. It is then baked or grilled, and usually served with a highly seasoned sauce.

SAINT-GERMAIN (san-zhaer-MAn) *Fr.* Dishes described this way will usually be made or garnished with peas, often puréed peas. POTAGE SAINT-GERMAIN (paw-TAHZH), for example, is purée of fresh green pea soup. Fillets of fish St.-Germain

103

are an exception. They are brushed with melted butter, rolled in bread crumbs, sprinkled with butter, and grilled. They are served with a Béarnaise sauce.

SAINT-HONORÉ (san-taw-naw-RAE) *Fr.* A tart or specialty cake, GÂTEAU (gah-TOH). The pastry shell is edged with balls of puff pastry which have been dipped in caramelized sugar. The pastry shell is filled with a custard cream—made with milk, eggs, sugar, a little flour, butter, and seasoned with vanilla—mixed with egg whites whipped with sugar. This dessert is named in honor of the patron saint of pastry cooks and bakers.

SAINT-HUBERT (san-tew-BAER) *Fr.* Saint Hubert, as we all know, was the patron saint of hunters. Dishes named in his honor will include game in one form or another. Classically, they are garnished with a purée of game in a brown sauce with a base of game broth.

SAISON (sae-ZAWN) *Fr.* Season. You may see this in two descriptions: DE SAISON (duh)—of the season, and EN SAISON (ahn)—in season.

SALAME, SALAMI (sah-LAH-mae, sah-LAH-mee) *It.* Sausages. They are usually made with ground or chopped pork and pork fat; other meats may occasionally be added. They may be seasoned with a wide variety of spices—some more, some less. Salame are dried, salted, and/or smoked.

SALAME GENOVESE (jae-noh-VAE-zae) The sausage of Genova (Genoa) is of the hard variety, served cold, sliced. It is made up of veal, pork, and pork fat, studded with peppercorns, and fairly highly spiced. The proportions are one-half veal, one-fifth pork, and one-third pork fat.

SALÉ (sa-LAE) *Fr.* Salted; corned of beef.

SALISBURY STEAK (SAWLS-bree) *Br.* A ground

beef patty, broiled or fried. Named for J. H. Salisbury, the nineteenth-century English dietitian.

SALMONE (sahl-MOH-nae) *It.* Salmon. And SALMONE AFFUMICATO (ahf-foo-mee-KAH-toh) or AFFUMATO (ahf-foo-MAH-toh) is none other than smoked salmon.

SALSA (SAHL-sah) *It.* Sauce, or gravy.

SALSICCIE (sahl-SEE-chae) *It.* Fresh pork sausages, as opposcd to the cured pork sausage called Salame.

SALTATO (sahl-TAH-toh) *It.* Sautéed. The term refers to the food's jumping or leaping ("saltare"—to jump, leap). Whether this is because sautéeing is done quickly and therefore the food practically leaps into and out of the pan, as it were, or if it describes the flipping of the food in the pan as it is turned over, is not clear—take your pick; it tastes the same.

SALTIMBOCCA (sahl-teem-BOHK-kah) *It.* Literally, jump into the mouth; presumably because these scallops of veal are so tempting that they do virtually that as you quickly snatch them up and pop them into your mouth. The veal is pounded thin and topped with thin slices of Prosciutto and sage leaf—some cooks substitute powdered sage. They are sautéed in butter, and often a little white wine or Marsala is mixed with the pan juices. A specialty of Rome.

SALVIA (SAHL-vyah) *It.* Sage.

SALZBURGER NOCKERL or NOCKERLN (ZAHLTS-boor-ger NOHK-erl or NOHK-erln) *Au.* The fluffy dessert of Salzburg, said to have been created there 250 years ago for the archbishop in the Hohensaltzburg castle high above the town. This is sort of a sweet soufflé made with eggs, milk, sugar, and a little flour, and sometimes butter, and flavored with vanilla or perhaps a little grated lemon rind. It may be dusted with confectioners' sugar.

SANS (sahn) *Fr.* Without.

SARDE, SARDELLE (SAHR-dae, sahr-DAEL-lae) *It.* Sardines.

SAUCISSES (soh-SEES) *Fr.* Fresh pork sausages.

SAUCISSON (soh-sees-SAWn) *Fr.* Pork sausages, cured, served sliced. They are made with pork and pork fat, with other kinds of meat occasionally added. Some are eaten uncooked, cold; others are heated up, or cooked, and served hot or cold.

SAUERBRATEN (ZOW-er-braht-en) *Gm.* Literally, a sour roast. This is a pot roast of beef which has been marinated in vinegar and water seasoned with onions, carrots, celery, cloves, peppercorns, and bay leaves. It is browned in fat and simmered in the marinade. Caramelized sugar is added to the gravy, sometimes also sour cream or gingersnaps, to produce a sweet and sour sauce. A specialty of the Rhineland. Potato dumplings, KARTOFFEL KLÖSSE (kahr-TOHF-fel KLUH-se), are the traditional accompaniment.

SAUGE (sohzh) *Fr.* Sage.

SAUMON (soh-MAWn) *Fr.* Salmon.

SAUMON FUMÉ (few-MAE) Smoked salmon. Served sliced, often with a garnish of capers. There are two types most often seen in American restaurants. Scotch salmon, ÉCOSSAIS (ae-kaw-SAE), is considered the best by gourmets; it is delicately flavored and not salty. Nova Scotia salmon, NOUVELLE-ÉCOSSE (noo-VEL-ae-KAWS), is brighter in color and stronger in flavor than Scotch salmon.

SAUTÉ (soh-TAE) *Fr.* Tossed in the pan; lightly fried in a small amount of fat.

SAUVAGE (soh-VAHZH) *Fr.* Wild, but not necessarily savage.

SAVOYARDE, À LA (sa-vwah-YARD) *Fr.* In the style of the province of Savoie, a cheese-producing region where gratin dishes are a specialty.

OMELETTE À LA SAVOYARDE (awm-LET) Thinly sliced potatoes fried in butter, mixed with grated Gruyère cheese and eggs, fried like a pancake omelette, that is, not folded over.

SCALOPPINE (skah-lohp-PEE-nae) *It.* Thin slices, or scallops, of veal pounded out flat; generally, if not always, sautéed.

SCAMPI (SKAHM-pee) *It.* The large shrimp, or prawns, of the Adriatic, a specialty of Venice. In American restaurants this name is used to describe a dish of broiled or sautéed shrimp in a sauce of garlic, butter, white wine and/or broth, often thickened with a little cornstarch or flour. Sometimes called Shrimp Scampi (shrimp shrimp).

SCAROLA (skah-ROH-lah) *It.* Escarole.

SCHLACHTPLATTE (SHLAHKT-plah-te) *Gm.* This is the "butcher's plate"—a selection of sausages and fresh or smoked meats; often accompanied by sauerkraut.

SCHNITZEL (SHNIHT-tsel) *Au., Gm.* Literally, a little slice (Schnitz) or chip. A thin slice—but not really small, it can be rather big around—of veal, often flattened further with a cutlet bat. Usually coated with egg and bread crumbs, but may be simply floured, as in NATURSCHNITZEL (nah-TEWR-shniht-tsel), and sautéed in butter.

HOLSTEINERSCHNITZEL (HOHL-shtiin-er-shniht-tsel) Schnitzel in the style of the German region Schleswig-Holstein. The veal is flattened and coated with flour, egg, and bread crumbs, and sautéed in butter; served topped with a fried or poached egg, and garnished with anchovy fillets, and often lemon slices, chopped or sliced beets and gherkins.

KALBSCHNITZEL (KAHLP-shniht-tsel) Veal schnitzel, usually called simply schnitzel.

RAHMSCHNITZEL (RAHM-shniht-tsel) Schnitzel floured and sautéed in butter, and served with a cream (rahm) sauce made with the pan juices mixed with cream and seasoned with paprika and perhaps a little mild mustard.

WIENERSCHNITZEL (VEEN-er-schniht-tsel) The Schnitzel of Wien (Vienna). The flattened veal slice is dipped in flour, egg, and bread crumbs, then sautéed in lard or butter. Generally served with lemon slices and parsley sprigs. According to the records, when the Austrian General Joseph Radetzky von Radetz was in Milano during the Italian campaign, the cuisine impressed him very much, especially the Scaloppine alla Milanese. He mentioned it in his reports to Vienna, and made it sound so good that the Emperor himself ordered the dish prepared by his chefs. It was a resounding success. So much so that the Viennese called it their own Schnitzel, Wienerschnitzel. Researchers have turned up evidence, however, that Milan wasn't even its original home, but that this cosmopolitan dish came to Italy from Spain with the troops of Emperor Charles V. A certain Cardinal Gattinari wrote of a "costoletta in the Spanish manner," which he had enjoyed. But if evidence should turn up showing that it had been introduced into Spain by the Romans (they did introduce winemaking there), well, we'd be right back in Italy again, wouldn't we? So far, of course, no one has uncovered any such evidence—but you never know!

SCOMBRO (SKOHM-broh) It. Mackerel.

SCUNGILLI (skoon-JEEL-lee) *It.* Conch. You know conch—that's the horn-like spiral shell you hold to your ear to listen to the sea. Well, the Italians don't just listen to it, they eat the meat as well. This is Neapolitan dialect for the Italian word "conchiglie," so you might expect a southern Italian treatment, such as a spicy sauce.

SEC, SÈCHE (sek, sesh) *Fr.* Dry, dried.

SECCO, SECCHI (SEK-koh, SEK-kee) *It.* Dry, dried.

SEDANO (SAE-dah-noh) *It.* Celery.

SELLE (sel) *Fr.* Saddle; a roast of both loins, often with kidneys.

SELON GROSSEUR (su-LAWn groh-SUHR) *Fr.* "According to size"—that's how it's priced.

SELVAGGINA (sel-vahj-JEE-nah) *It.* Game.

SEPPIE (SAEP-pyae) *It.* Cuttlefish, inkfish.

SERVICE COMPRIS (saer-VEES kawn-PREE) *Fr.* Service charge included in the prices charged. (But if you feel like leaving a tip on top of that, it's up to you).

SFOGLIE (SFOH-lyae) *It.* Sole.

PASTA SFOGLIE (PAH-stah) This, though, means flaky pastry; it is sometimes called simply Sfoglie, or Sfogliatelle.

S. G. See Selon Grosseur.

SGOMBRO (SGOHM-broh) *It.* Mackerel.

SHASHLIK (shahsh-LEEK) *Rs.* Cubes of lamb grilled on a skewer, over a charcoal fire sometimes. This is a dish of rather humble beginnings, in the Caucasus mountains. It seems those rough and ready types from that region in earlier times would spear hunks of meat with their swords and hold them over the open fire to cook. (Could this have been the beginning of sword swallowing as well?) Shashlik is still sometimes served spitted on a sword, a flaming sword in restaurants with a flair for the dramatic. The chunks of meat (sometimes beef) are marinated in olive oil, lemon juice, and onion, or perhaps red wine, and threaded on skewers with onion and bay leaves.

SHIRRED EGGS Eggs broken into shallow—often individual—casserole dishes lined with melted butter, the eggs sprinkled with more butter and baked.

SHISH KEBAB See Kabob, Kebab.

SICILIANA, ALLA (see-chee-LYAH-nah) *It.* In the style of Sicily (Sicilia), where eggplant is a favorite vegetable and anchovy a favorite seasoning. Dishes described as in the Sicilian style will often, in America, be cooked (this doesn't include desserts, by the way) with a sauce of garlic, and diced or sliced eggplant cooked in olive oil, and chopped tomatoes, anchovy, often capers and black olives, sometimes peppers, pimientos, and/or celery, and spiced with basil or oregano. Parmesan—or in Sicily, the local Caciocavallo cheese—may be grated over the top, especially if this is a pasta dish. MELANZANE ALLA SICILIANA (mae-lahn-DZAH-nae) Multiply the eggplant in proportion to the rest of the sauce, bake it in a casserole, and you get Eggplant alla Siciliana. Often served cold. That's in American restaurants. In Sicily, Melanzane alla Siciliana is a little different—chopped eggplant, black olives, anchovy fillets, tomatoes, and capers sprinkled with black pepper and drizzled with olive oil are baked in the scooped-out halves of the eggplant.

SMITANE (smee-TAN) *Fr.* A sauce of sautéed onion, white wine, and sour cream, with perhaps a dash of lemon juice. This French sauce is of Russian origin, where "smetana" means sour cream.

SOFT-SHELL CRABS Crabs which have just shed

their outgrown hard shells and have a papery soft new one. They are usually floured and sautéed in butter. They are eaten shell and all (it's tender, not even crispy).

SOGLIOLA (SOH-lyoh-lah) *It.* Sole.

SOGLIOLA INGLESE (een-GLAE-zae) This is not a method of preparing sole—it means simply English, or Dover, sole.

SORBET (sawr-BAE) *Fr.* A frozen dessert made with puréed fruit and/or liqueurs with sugar syrup and whipped egg whites.

SORPRESA, OMELETTE (oh-mae-LAET-tae sohr-PRAE-zah) *It.* This "surprise omelette" is better known as Baked Alaska, which see.

SOTT-OLIO (soht-OH-lyoh) *It.* Under the oil, in oil.

SOUFFLÉ (soo-FLAE) *Fr.* Literally, puffed up. This is a light dish, the main ingredient of which is eggs. The whites are whipped to a froth and mixed with the yolks, often a white sauce (flour, butter, and milk), and the particular flavoring—grated cheese, puréed poultry or fish or vegetable. Or, if it's a dessert Soufflé, sugar is added to the eggs and cream or milk, flour, and butter mix, and a fruit purée and/or flavorings—chocolate, lemon, almond, or whatever—are added. This term is also sometimes used for another airy dish, Mousseline, which see; and for frozen chiffon-type desserts made to resemble a Soufflé.

SOUS CLOCHE (soo klawsh) *Fr.* Under a bell, a glass bell. See Under Glass.

SOUTHERN FRIED CHICKEN (SU-thun frahd CHIH-kihn) The pieces of chicken are rolled in flour, sometimes seasoned with a little cinnamon, and fried in lard or shortening. A gravy is made from some of the pan fat mixed with flour and milk or cream, and poured over the chicken.

SOUVAROFF, SOUVAROV, À LA (soo-va-RAWF, soo-VOHR-owv) *Fr.* A method of preparing poultry and game birds, notably pheasant, FAISAN (fu-ZAɴ). The bird is stuffed with chopped foie gras and truffles, seasoned with salt and pepper and brandy, then cooked in butter. The cooking juices are mixed with a little Madeira and broth laced with a little more brandy, and large slices of truffles are added. Then the lid is sealed on the pot with a flour and water paste—to keep all the juices and flavors in—and it is baked in the earthenware casserole.

SPANISH OMELETTE There are two types of Spanish omelette: Spanish Spanish Omelette, or Tortilla à la Española, which see, and American Spanish Omelette. The American omelette has nothing in common with the Spanish except the name—and the eggs, of course. Well, also the onions too, but believe me, there's a big difference. For the American omelette, chopped onions, sweet pepper or chili pepper, tomato, and sometimes celery, olives, parsley and/or mushrooms as well, are sautéed and the beaten eggs are added.

SPEZZATINO (spae-tsah-TEE-noh) *It.* Literally, broken up or cut into little pieces. This is stew.

SPEZZATO (spae-TSAH-toh) *It.* Cut up and cooked in a sauce.

SPIEDINI (spyae-DEE-nee) *It.* Spitted; broiled or grilled on skewers.
SPIEDINO ALLA ROMANA The skewered specialty of Rome is cheese crusts on a skewer, also known as Crostini alla Romana, which see, under Romana.

SPIEDO, AL (SPYAE-doh) *It.* On the spit, skewered.

SPIGOLA (SPEE-goh-lah) *It.* Striped bass, sea bass.

SPUMONE (spoo-MOH-nae) *It.* Neapolitan ice

cream. Not the chocolate-vanilla-strawberry number in stripes of ordinary ice cream, although that's probably an imitation of the original Naples specialty. This is a light, foamy ("spuma"—foam, froth) ice cream made with egg whites or whipped cream. In America it's called SPUMONI (spoo-MOH-nee) and combines a variety of flavors—vanilla, chocolate, strawberry, and/or pistachio—with bits of fruit, especially maraschino cherry and perhaps pistachio nuts or almonds.

SQUAB   A fledgling pigeon. The term is also used for a very young tender chicken weighing about one pound, but usually in that case it's qualified—Squab Chicken.

STAGIONE, DI (dee stah-JOH-nae) *It.* In season, of the season.

STECCHE, ALLE (AHL-lae STAEK-kae) *It.* Literally, on sticks—grilled on skewers.

STORIONE (stoh-RYOH-nae) *It.* Sturgeon.

STRACCIATELLA (strah-chah-TAEL-lah) *It.* Literally, little rags. This soup is a specialty of Rome. A mixture of eggs, grated Parmesan cheese, a little flour, sometimes seasoned with nutmeg or lemon peel, or perhaps chopped parsley, is beaten into boiling broth—usually chicken broth—which breaks it into strands or "tatters."

STRACCIATELLA ALLA FIORENTINA (fyoh-raen-TEE-nah) Naming this soup after Firenza (Florence) indicates the addition of spinach.

STRACOTTO (strah-KOHT-toh) *It.* Literally, overcooked. This is slowly cooked braised meat, or pot roast.

STRASBOURGEOISE, A LA (stras-boor-ZHWAHZ) *Fr.* Describing a dish as in the style of Strasbourg, a town famous for its geese—and their overstuffed livers, foie gras—and for its sausage (similar to the frankfurter), usually means that Strasbourg sausages or foie gras will be included in the dish.

STROGANOFF, STROGANOV (STROH-gah-nawf) *Rs.* A style of preparing beef which is cut into thin strips and sautéed in butter with sliced or chopped onion and often mushrooms and combined with a sauce of sour cream and meat broth—some cooks add red wine—seasoned with a dash of lemon juice and a little mustard; sometimes chopped pickles and/or paprika are also added. Generally served over egg noodles. Said to be named for the nineteenth-century Russian count and diplomat credited with creating the dish.

STRUDEL (SHTREW-dul) *Au.* The flaky pastry of Austria, known in France as Millefeuille, and in Italy as Millefoglie and Sfogliatelle. It was introduced into Europe by the Saracens. (They weren't all bad). This paper-thin pastry is filled usually, but not necessarily, with a sweet filling, rolled up and baked.

APFELSTRUDEL (AHP-fel) For this, the pastry is filled with a mixture of chopped apples sprinkled with sugar and other goodies such as walnuts or almonds, raisins or currants, and bits of candied citron. It is often seasoned with cinnamon and dusted with confectioners' sugar.

STUFATINO, STUFATO (stoo-fah-TEE-noh, stoo-FAH-toh) *It.* Stewed or braised meat.

SUCCO (SOOK-koh) *It.* Juice.

SUCRE (sewkr) *Fr.* Sugar.

SUGO, AL (SOO-goh) *It.* With gravy or sauce, usually meat sauce if the word is used alone, unqualified.

SUPPLÌ AL TELEFONO (soop-PLEE ahl tae-LAE-foh-noh) *It.* These "croquettes on the telephone" are a specialty of Rome. They are made of risotto—rice cooked in meat broth, butter, and grated Parmesan cheese—bound together with eggs. The rice mixture is formed into balls stuffed with cubes of cheese, Provatura or, usually, Mozzarella, and often chopped ham (Prosciutto), then rolled in bread crumbs and deep fried in oil. Sometimes they are made with a richer filling: besides the cheese and ham, chopped chicken livers, mushrooms, ground meat, onions, sweetbread, and tomatoes, sautéed in butter. When the rice croquette is cut into, the cheese stretches out between the two pieces in strands suggesting telephone wires.

SUPRÊME (sew-PRAEM) *Fr.* This is the cut of poultry, DE VOLAILLE (duh vaw-LAHY), considered supreme, or the best part—the breast, skinless and boneless; sometimes flattened, sometimes cut into fillets. Originally it was just the wing, then the wing and breast, now it's just the breast. The term Suprême is used for chicken and other birds, and even sometimes for fillets of veal or of sole, but not often. The Suprêmes may or may not be served with SAUCE SUPRÊME (sohs). This sauce is made with a base of flour and butter to which chicken broth, sometimes egg yolk, and heavy cream are added, seasoned with an optional dash of lemon juice.

SURPRISE, OMELETTE Another name for Baked Alaska, which see.

SWEETBREAD You thought maybe it was bread? Well, it isn't sweet either. There are two kinds of sweetbreads: the one from the throat of the lamb or the calf—thymus, and the one from the chest, pancreas. The throat sweetbread is a longer oval in

115

shape; the one from the chest, more rounded, is considered by gourmets the better of the two.

TABLE D'HÔTE (tabl doht) *Fr.* Literally, the host's table. The house dinner or lunch, with prearranged courses at a fixed price.

TACCHINO (tahk-KEE-noh) *It.* Turkey.

TAGLIATELLE (tah-lyah-TAEL-lae) *It.* The ribbon noodles of Bologna—called in Rome, Fettuccine—about ¼ to ½ inch wide. Tagliatelle (from "tagliare"—to cut) is supposed to have been created by a Bolognese chef inspired by Lucrezia Borgia's blond tresses at the banquet in celebration of her marriage to the Duke of Este. It seems an unfortunate connection to bring up, what with her alleged dabbling in poison, but it was her hair, that inspired him, not the things she cooked up.

TAPAS (TAH-pahs) *Sp.* Hors d'oeuvres; tidbits such as olives, shrimp, GAMBAS (GAHM-bahs), pieces of TORTILLA (torh-TEE-yah), to munch as you sip a Sherry, JEREZ (he-RETH).

TARGONE (tahr-GOH-nae) *It.* Tarragon.

TARTARE, STEAK TARTARE (tar-TAR) *Fr.* Twice-ground, raw lean beef, served shaped into a mound, often with a raw egg yolk set into a well in the top. It is garnished with chopped raw onion, parsley, and capers, and perhaps other seasonings. You mix in the egg and the seasonings of your choice. This dish is named for the barbarian Tartars, who apparently hadn't yet reached that stage of civilization where they cooked their meat—or maybe they were just too busy wreaking havoc.
À LA TARTARE This usually means the dish is served with Sauce Tartare, but BIFTECK À LA TARTARE (bihf-TEK) is another name for Steak Tartare.

SAUCE TARTARE (sohs) A cold sauce, usually served with fish, made of egg yolk whipped with oil seasoned with a little wine vinegar, white wine, Dijon mustard, chopped parsley, perhaps tarragon, chives, or shallots, and chopped gherkins.

TARTE (tart) *Fr.* An open, single-crust, pie; a tart. The filling may be sweet or savory, usually sweet.

TARTUFATO (tahr-too-FAH-toh) *It.* Truffled, made with truffles.

TARTUFI (tahr-TOO-fee) *It.* Truffles. Italian truffles may be either black or white. Piemonte (Piedmont) is famous for its white truffles, which are eaten raw, and added at the last minute to hot dishes. The region of Umbria produces most of Italy's black truffles.

TASSE, EN (ahn tas) *Fr.* In a cup.

TAZZA, IN (een TAT-tsah) *It.* In a cup.

TÈ (tae) *It.* Tea.

TERRINE (te-REEN) *Fr.* This is similar to Pâté, which see. The names are often used interchangeably although there is a difference. The original Pâtés were baked in pastry crust and sometimes still are; Terrines are not. A Terrine is baked in an earthenware dish called a terrine, which is lined with pork fat. The mixture for a Terrine is the same as for a pâté: ground fish, poultry, or meat(s), and pork fat (the fat used with fish is butter), and sometimes liver, seasoned with spices and often brandy, sometimes nuts or even truffles. Sometimes the fat which surrounds the Terrine is replaced (after cooking) with aspic. Terrine is served sliced and often garnished with lettuce, gherkins, and/or a sprig of parsley; sometimes with chopped aspic or a particular sauce.

THÉ (tae) *Fr.* Tea.

THERMIDOR (taer-mee-DAWR) *Fr.* A style of

117

preparing lobster, HOMARD (aw-MAR). The meat is cut up, returned to the shell, and baked in a sauce made with cream or milk, often chopped shallots or scallions and mushrooms sautéed in butter, fish or lobster broth, usually white wine, sometimes laced with brandy, seasoned with mustard and perhaps a touch of hot pepper or a little tarragon, sometimes a dash of lemon juice, and often thickened with flour and butter or egg yolks. On top is a crust of grated cheese sometimes mixed with buttered bread crumbs. Thermidor was the eleventh month of the calendar of the first French republic, falling in midsummer—as good a time as any to enjoy this dish.

THON (tawn) *Fr.* Tuna, or tunny fish.

TIMBALE, TIMBALLO (tan-BAL) *Fr.* (teem-BAHL-loh) *It.* Literally, kettle drum. Originally this was, and sometimes still is, a pastry crust with high sides filled with meat, poultry, fish, and/or vegetables in a sauce. It may also be a molded custard made with meat, poultry, or fish and/or vegetables, cooked in a timbale dish (in the shape of the original pastry crust) often lined with rice or macaroni, and turned out to form a dome or kettle drum shape when served. Or it may be a combination of foods formed into a timbale shape when served.

TONNATO, VITELLO (vee-TAEL-loh tohn-NAH-toh) *It.* Cold veal in tuna sauce. The veal roast is simmered in white wine and water seasoned with onions, carrots, tuna fish, and anchovy fillets. Sometimes celery, bay leaf, and parsley are also added. The meat is then cooled and sliced thin. The sauce is made from the cooking broth plus olive oil, egg yolk, and perhaps a little lemon juice and cream, which are whipped together, then capers are added. The sauce is spread over the cold slices of veal, and the dish garnished with lemon slices and perhaps black olives.

TONNO (TOHN-noh) *It.* Tuna, tunny fish.

TORRONE (tohr-ROH-nae) *It.* Nougat. It is made from egg whites, honey, sugar, and roasted nuts. Sometimes flavored with chocolate, lemon, candied fruits, and the like. It is covered with (edible) rice paper. Torrone is supposed to have been invented in Cremona. At the banquet celebrating the wedding of Bianca Maria Visconti and Francesco Sforza, the dessert created in honor of the occasion was a replica in nougat of Cremona's twelfth-century campanile, the Torrazzo, which is also how, according to the people of Cremona, the nougat came to be named "Torrone."

TORTA (TOHR-tah) *It.* Tart, which see.

TORTELLINI (tohr-tael-LEE-nee) *It.* These "small twists" are rings of egg pasta stuffed with ground meat, cheese, and spices. In Bologna, where they are a specialty, they are stuffed with a filling which may be considered a classic filling for Tortellini: ground veal, Prosciutto, Mortadella (a pork sausage), and grated Parmesan cheese, seasoned with a sprinkling of nutmeg. The legend in Bologna has it that the shape of this pasta was inspired by a feminine navel—Venus's or the navel of the creator's lady love depending on which version you prefer. Tortellini may be served in consommé, IN BRODO (een BROH-doh), under a sauce, or just topped with melted butter and grated Parmesan cheese.

TORTILLA (tohr-TEE-yah) What a Tortilla is depends on the restaurant you're in—whether it's Spanish or Mexican. Tortilla á la Española, also known as Spanish Omelette, is crusty on the outside and moist on the inside. Chopped onions and potatoes are sautéed in olive oil, sometimes flavored with garlic, and stirred into beaten eggs, then fried in oil to a crusty brown. This is cut into wedges and served hot or cold. Other vegetables may be added—asparagus, mushrooms, etc.—or shellfish such as shrimp, or meat—sausages, ham—but these additions to the classic tortilla should be indicated in the name. For example, CON JAMÓN (kohn hah-MOHN)—with ham; CON GAMBAS (GAHM-bahs)—with prawns or shrimp. The Mexican Tortilla is another story. This is a thin, flat corn cake—the bread of pre-Columbian Mexico. It is made simply with corn flour and water, and cooked on a hot griddle—originally, a hot stone, no doubt—without any grease. The recipe has been handed down through the centuries unchanged. Traditionally, salt is not even added to the dough. Tortillas may be fried crisp, and if rolled, may be used as a scoop for Guacamole or Chili.

TORTONI or BISCUIT TORTONI (bees-KWEE tohr-TOH-nee) *It.* A frozen dessert made with whipped egg whites and cream (also whipped) mixed with sugar, milk, macaroon crumbs, almond liqueur, and vanilla. Tortoni usually are served in little paper cups and are topped with more macaroon ("amaretti") crumbs. These desserts are named for their creator, Signor Tortoni, a Neapolitan whose café in Paris flourished in the late eighteenth century.

TORTUE (tawr-TEW) *Fr.* Turtle, tortoise.

TOURNEDOS (toor-nu-DOH) *Fr.* A thick slice of beef from the filet, or tenderloin, usually sautéed in butter and/or oil, although it may be broiled. The theory is that the name is based on the fact that these tender little steaks should be quickly cooked, so quickly in fact that if you turn (tourner) your back (dos), they will be done before you can snatch them out of the pan.

TOURNEDOS ROSSINI (rohs-SEE-nee) This recipe for Tournedos is supposed to have been created by the famous Italian composer Gioacchino Rossini, who was also something of a gourmet, and living in Paris. The Tournedos is sautéed in butter, and served on a crustless piece of fried bread. It is topped with a slice of foie gras garnished with sliced truffles, and a sauce of Madeira and beef broth combined with the pan juices.

TOUT PARFUMS (too par-FUHN) *Fr.* All flavors.

TRANCHE (transh) *Fr.* Slice.

TRENETTE (trae-NET-tae) *It.* The thin ribbon noodles of Liguria.

TRIFLE, *Br.* An English dessert. This is lady fingers, or fingers of sponge cake, spread with fruit jam, soaked with Sherry or perhaps rum or brandy, and topped with a rich custard, made with milk or cream, sugar, and perhaps a little flour, mixed with beaten eggs and sometimes flavored with vanilla or almond extract, perhaps a dash of lemon juice, and topped with toasted almonds, or perhaps candied fruit.

TRIFOLATO (tree-foh-LAH-toh) *It.* Foods described this way are sliced very thin, and often sautéed; sometimes with a sauce, sometimes without. The word itself may be derived from the dialect word for truffles, "trifola," and refer to the very thin slices which truffles are often pared into.

TRIPPA (TREEP-pah) *It.* Tripe.

TROTA (TROH-tah) *It.* Trout.

TROTTERS   The British term for the feet that we put in our mouths on purpose—that is, pig's feet and sheep's feet.

TRUFFÉ (trew-FAE) *Fr.* Truffled, made with truffles.

TRUFFES (trewf) *Fr.* Truffles.

TRUFFLES   This crowning touch of haute cuisine is a variety of underground (you should forgive the expression) fungus. There are both black and white varieties. The Périgord region of southern France is famous for black truffles; the Piedmont in northern Italy, for white ones. Italy also produces black truffles, in Umbria, a region of central Italy. In France a special breed of pig is used (the sows especially) for sniffing out and rooting up the truffles, which grow around the roots of trees, chiefly oak trees. In Italy, dogs are favored for truffle hunting and there is even a school for training them. It is said that mongrel dogs make the best truffle hounds. The obedient dogs find the truffles for their masters, dig them up, and go on to the next. When the pigs, on the other hand, have rooted out the truffles, their masters sometimes have a tussle with them to see who gets possession. (They're not called pigs for nothing!) The pigs are offered a consolation prize: an acorn or the like. The hunt takes place at night; they say the scent of the truffles is stronger then. But it might also have something to do with secrecy, as the truffles grow in the same favored—you might even say charmed—spots year after year. Truffles can be cooked in many ways, but are usually thinly sliced or chopped, sautéed (black truffles), and added to sauces or dishes to heighten the flavors. The white ones are eaten raw or very slightly cooked, being added at the last moment of cooking. Truffles have a strong perfume but an elusive flavor. They have the effect of enriching the flavors of the foods that they are added to.

TRUITE (trweet) *Fr.* Trout.

TRUITE DE RIVIÈRE (duh ree-VYAER) Brook trout.

TURKISH COFFEE This strong brew is made of coffee beans ground to a powder, sugar, and water boiled together till it foams, the foam being considered an essential part of the coffee. The amount of sugar used tends to be quite generous. When the coffee is poured into a cup, the grounds sink to the bottom and shouldn't be stirred up. The Turks, or Saracens, introduced coffee to Europe. Well, maybe introduced isn't quite the word. It seems that when the Saracens were defeated in their attempt to take Vienna in 1683, they left behind in their flight bags of coffee beans. From this, the Viennese got their first taste of Kaffee—and perhaps toasted their victory with cups of the refreshing beverage. The first coffeehouses in Europe, though, according to other sources, were a little farther south, in Venice to be exact. It seems the Venetian ambassador had become acquainted with the coffee-drinking habit of the Turks in Constantinople in the sixteenth century. Cafés and coffeehouses sprang up like mushrooms all over Europe in the seventeenth century.

TUTTO GIARDINO (TOOT-toh jahr-DEE-noh) *It.* Literally, the whole garden. This refers to a dish made with a variety of mixed vegetables.

UCCELLETTI (oo-chael-LAET-tee) *It.* This might mean small birds (including song birds), but is also used for beef or veal "birds"—a more likely translation in America, where we might tend to feel bad for the poor little birds. Thin slices of meat, pounded flat, and rolled up around a stuffing such as Prosciutto and spices, they are sometimes grilled on a skewer as small birds often are in Italy (probably the origin of the name), or they might be braised.

UMIDO, AL' or IN (een OO-mee-doh) *It.* You might think this means steamed—"humid," right? Wrong; it means stewed in liquid.

UNDER GLASS Under a glass bell. The food is cooked covered with a glass bell which allows it to steam in its own juices. The glass bell is often removed just at serving time, giving the diner the scent of the cooking aromas as they are first released. Similar to the effect of cooking in a bag of greaseproof paper, which is opened by the diner in a puff of aromatic steam, but rather more elegant.

UOVA (WOH-vah) *It.* Eggs.

ALL'UOVO (ahl WOH-voh) When pasta is described this way—with egg—it means egg noodles, made with eggs and flour (rather than water and flour, as Macaroni is), not served with an egg sauce, as it might appear at first glance.

UVA (OO-vah) *It.* Grapes.

UVA PASSA or SECCA (PAHS-sah, SAEK-kah) "Dried grapes," raisins.

VALDOSTANA, ALLA (vahl-doh-STAH-nah) *It.* In the style of the Valle d'Aosta or Val d'Aosta, that little Alpine region in the northwestern corner of Italy. A specialty of that region is COSTOLETTA DI VITELLO CON FONTINA (koh-stoh-LAET-tah dee vee-TAEL-loh kohn fohn-TEE-nah), also called Costoletta alla Valdostana. This is veal chops stuffed with Fontina cheese, dusted with flour, dipped in beaten egg and bread crumbs, and sautéed in butter. Some restaurants add Prosciutto to the stuffing, and sometimes slices of white truffles enrich the dish. Sliced mushrooms are another addition occasionally made. As for substitutions, Mozzarella is often used in place of the Fontina, especially in the United States. Chicken breasts, PETTI DI POLLO (PAET-tee dee POHL-loh), may be used instead of veal, and this will naturally be indicated in the name. The chicken is sometimes served with a sauce of white wine mixed with the pan juices and Madeira, or perhaps cream. Some restaurants serve the veal chops with a gravy also. A lot of liberties are taken with this dish outside of Valle d'Aosta; to many chefs the original recipe serves merely as a point of departure.

VAPEUR, À LA (va-PUHR) *Fr.* Steamed, in the vapor.

VEAL BIRDS These are slices of veal, pounded out flat, spread with a stuffing of some kind, rolled up, and tied. They are browned in butter or oil, then simmered in a little liquid.

VEAU (voh) *Fr.* Veal.

VELOUTÉ (vu-loo-TAE) *Fr.* This "velvety" sauce is made with flour, butter, and broth. This may be meat, chicken, or fish broth, depending on what kind of food it is to be served with. Sometimes milk or cream and occasionally egg yolks enrich the sauce. Velouté soups, POTAGES VELOUTÉS (paw-TAHZH), are made with a base of Velouté sauce. The meat, chicken, fish, or vegetable which the soup is named for is puréed and the soup is enriched with egg yolks, butter, and cream.

VELLUTATO DI (vael-loo-TAH-toh dee) *It.* Literally, velvet of; we would say, cream of.

VENAISON (vu-nae-ZAWɴ) *Fr.* Venison.

VENEZIANA, ALLA (vae-nae-TSYAH-nah) *It.* In

125

the style of Venezia (Venice), meaning simply however the dish is prepared in that city.

FEGATO ALLA VENEZIANA (FAE-gah-toh) This is calf's liver sliced paper thin and quickly sautéed in oil and butter with thinly sliced onions which have been cooking more slowly to a golden color. It is sprinkled with chopped parsley, salt, and pepper, and traditionally served with Polenta, which see.

VÉNITIENNE (vae-nee-SYEN) *Fr.* A French sauce named for an Italian city, Venice. It is made with chopped shallots, chervil, tarragon, and parsley, a little wine vinegar, flour, butter, and broth (which kind depends on the dish it will be served with), egg yolk, and perhaps a little puréed spinach.

VERDE (VAER-dae) *It.* Green. Green pasta gets its color (if it's made authentically, and let's assume it is) from puréed spinach added to the pasta dough.

VERDURA (vaer-DOO-rah) *It.* Greens, vegetables.

VERMICELLI (vaer-mee-CHAEL-lee) *It.* Literally, little worms, but don't let that discourage you. This is extra thin spaghetti.

VÉRONIQUE (vae-ru-NEEK) *Fr.* Dishes prepared in this style will be garnished with white grapes (Veronica's favorite fruit?). The classic dish is SOLE VÉRONIQUE. The fillets of sole are poached in white wine and fish broth, and served with a sauce made with the poaching liquor thickened with flour and butter and a little cream. The dish is garnished, of course, with white grapes.

VERT, VERTE (vaer, vaert) *Fr.* Green.

SAUCE VERTE (sohs) Made with mayonnaise greened with puréed spinach, watercress, parsley, chives, and tarragon (some or all of these).

VERT-PRÉ (vaer-prae) *Fr.* Literally, green meadow. Dishes prepared in this style will usually be served with watercress and Maître d'Hôtel butter. Occassionally, as in fish dishes, this may mean served with Sauce Verte (containing watercress).

VIANDE (vyahnd) *Fr.* Meat.

VICHY, À LA (vee-SHEE) *Fr.* In the style of Vichy. A preparation for carrots, CAROTTES (ka-RAWT) (carrots being considered at one time, like the spa's water, to be good for the liver). The carrots are sliced and boiled in water with butter, sugar, and sometimes a dash of lemon juice, and perhaps a pinch of bicarbonate of soda, unless Vichy water is being used. The glazed carrots are sprinkled with chopped parsley.

VICHYSSOISE (vee-shee-SWAHZ) This is not exactly a French soup, having been created in America. It was created by a Frenchman, though—Louis Diat, then head chef at New York City's Ritz-Carlton. It is an elegant variation on the classic French leek and potato soup, and named for his native Vichy. Vichyssoise is made with potatoes and the white part of leeks, sometimes also onion, cooked in butter and chicken broth, or water, enriched with cream and perhaps milk, seasoned with salt and white pepper, puréed and chilled. Served with a sprinkling of chopped chives, although some restaurants may substitute chopped parsley.

VILLEROI, À LA (veel-RWAH) *Fr.* Dishes prepared in this style are coated with a thick Villeroi sauce, dipped in egg and crumbs, and fried in oil.

SAUCE VILLEROI (sohs) Made with butter, flour, broth, egg yolks, cream or milk, and flavored with mushrooms.

VIN BLANC, AU (oh van blahn) *Fr.* This may mean simply in white wine, but may also mean in Sauce Vin Blanc.

MAQUEREAU AU VIN BLANC (ma-KROH) The mackerel is poached in white wine and water flavored with seasonings such as onions, peppercorns, bay leaf, lemon peel, and perhaps a little fennel. The fillets are chilled and served in this broth garnished with chopped parsley.

SAUCE VIN BLANC (sohs) Made with butter, fish broth, egg yolks, sometimes flour, and perhaps cream, often seasoned with lemon juice and maybe a little bit of mushroom.

VINAIGRETTE (vee-nae-GRET) *Fr.* Vinegar (vinaigre—literally, sour wine) sauce for cold foods, especially vegetables and salad. Vinaigrette is a simple French dressing made with oil, especially olive oil, wine vinegar (lemon juice is sometimes substituted, but belies the name), salt, and pepper. That's it, though many chefs will add a little Dijon mustard, which gives it a cloudy look. Chopped garlic, shallots, or scallions may also be added, and sometimes chopped herbs such as tarragon and parsley.

VITELLO (vee-TAEL-loh) *It.* Veal.

VOLAILLE (vaw-LAHY) *Fr.* Poultry, usually chicken.

VOL-AU-VENT (vawl-oh-VAHN) Fr. Literally, flight in the wind. This is a light, airy, puff pastry—so light in fact that, if you can believe the name, a gust of wind would sweep it right away. These pastries are scooped out and used as cases to hold chunks of chicken, seafood, mushrooms, and the like in cream sauces.

VONGOLE (VOHN-goh-lae) *It.* The little clams of Rome and southern Italy. But in American restaurants the word is generally used for hard-shelled clams, little necks.

WALDORF SALAD This salad, named for the Waldorf Astoria Hotel in New York City, where it was created, is a combination of chopped apples, celery, and walnuts tossed with a mayonnaise dressing.

WALEWSKA, À LA (vah-LEF-skah) *Fr.* This is a style of preparing fish, especially SOLE. The fillets are poached, then topped with pieces of lobster or rock lobster meat and slices of truffle. Mornay sauce and butter creamed with lobster coral, and sometimes pounded shells (sieved) and lobster meat, is spread on the top and the sauce browned under a flame. Named perhaps for Napoleon's Polish mistress, Countess Marie Walewska.

WATERZOOÏ (va-ter-ZOOY) *Bl.* This national dish of Belgium is a Flemish fish stew, which originated in the city of Ghent. Chunks of freshwater fish—two or three different kinds, sometimes including eel—are poached in a broth seasoned with chopped celery, and perhaps onions, cooked in butter, and herbs such as parsley, thyme, bay leaf, and perhaps sage, clove, or fennel, and sometimes a little white wine. The broth is dotted with butter and thickened with bread crumbs. It is generally served with toast or bread and butter.

CHICKEN WATERZOOÏ Cut-up chicken, sometimes browned in butter, and cooked with carrots, onions, leeks, celery, and sometimes garlic in broth and white wine seasoned with a little lemon juice, bay leaf, parsley and cloves, and thickened with bread crumbs, or perhaps egg yolk or cream. Generally served with toast or boiled potatoes.

WELLINGTON, BEEF or STEAK, *Br.* This is a filet steak or, if Beef Wellington, a whole fillet or tenderloin, partially roasted, then spread with pâté de foie gras or sometimes a mixture of sautéed chopped mushrooms and perhaps with shallots and Madeira combined with foie gras, wrapped in a pastry crust and baked. It is served sliced, often with a rich sauce of meat broth, Madeira, and chopped truffles. Said to have been a favorite of the Duke of Wellington, and presumably named in his honor.

WESTERN OMELETTE An omelette containing chopped ham, onions, and green peppers.

WORCESTERSHIRE (WOOR-ster-sher, WOOR-ster-sheer) *Br.* A commercially bottled sauce made with vinegar, water, molasses, soy, sugar, anchovy, tamarinds, onions, garlic, shallots, salt, spices, and flavorings. It is, as it says on the label, made "from the recipe of a nobleman in the county" (Worcester). According to the story, an ex-governor of Bengal invented the sauce in the 1830s to go with Indian food. Back in England, he took his recipe to Mr. Lea and Mr. Perrins in Worcester, who mixed up a batch for him. He didn't care for the results, however, and left it there. The barrel sat in the cellar for some time before it was come across by Mr. Lea or Mr. Perrins—well, probably an underling—cleaning out the cellar. They tasted the aged sauce and were so impressed they put it on the market as Worcestershire Sauce under their name.

WÜRST, WÜRSTCHEN (vewrst, VEWRST-shen) *Gm.* Sausage, little sausage—fresh or cured.

BLUTWÜRST (BLOOT-vewrst) blood sausage, made with pork, pork fat, onion, and of course pig's blood, seasoned generally with a little ginger and cloves.

BOCKWÜRST (BAWK-vewrst) A fresh sausage of veal, pork, pork fat, egg, and milk, seasoned with onion or leeks, chives, and perhaps a little parsley and nutmeg.

BRATWÜRST (BRAHT-vewrst) A fresh sausage for frying (braten) made with pork, veal, sometimes bread crumbs, and seasoned with a little nutmeg and mace or sage, and perhaps a dash of lemon juice.

KNACKWÜRST, KNOCKWÜRST (NAHK-vewrst, NAWK-vewrst) Smoked sausage made with pork, pork fat, beef, and seasoned with garlic, saltpeter (for color), and cumin.

WEISSWÜRST (VIIS-vewrst) Fresh "white" sausages of Munich made with veal, egg, white bread soaked in milk, and seasoned with a little lemon peel, parsley, and perhaps nutmeg.

WIENERWÜRSTCHEN (VEE-ner-vewrst-shen) *Au.* Little sausages of Vienna (Wien), very similar to the sausages of Frankfurt-am-Main, except smaller—made from beef and pork and mildly spiced. This must be where the term wieners, or wienies, came from.

XÉRÈS, AU (oh ksae-RES) *Fr.* With Sherry, the famous fortified wine of the Andalusian town of Jerez.

YAOURT (ya-OORT) *Fr.* Yogurt, sometimes offered on the cheese plate.

YORKSHIRE PUDDING (YAWRK-shur, YAWRK-sheer) *Br.* This doesn't have much in common with the American idea of a pudding, but in England the word seems to have a far wider meaning. Yorkshire pudding is a batter of flour, milk (sometimes mixed with water), and beaten eggs which is baked in the oven in the drippings from a roast, traditionally under a roast beef to catch the meat juices. The batter puffs up almost like a soufflé. This was the creation of a cook in Yorkshire in northern England. It is usually now cooked separately, alas, not under the meat. And often it is made in individual portions, and what you are served is actually a sort of a popover.

ZABAGLIONE, ZABAIONE (dzah-bah-LYOH-nae, dzah-bah-YOH-nae) *It.* This rich custard is often whipped up tableside. Generally it is made of egg yolks, sugar, and Marsala beaten together over a burner until it thickens to a pudding consistency. This is what you might call the classic dish, the one generally served. But it may be varied; the Marsala may be replaced by white wine and vanilla, lemon or orange rind, or liqueurs. This would still be Zabaglione, though it's not too often you'll see it in America—in Italy perhaps. Zabaglione may be served hot of cold.

ZITI (DZEE-tee) *It.* These "bridegrooms" may be either long tubular macaroni (especially in Naples, where it's a favorite) or short cuts of tubular macaroni (especially in America).

ZUCCHERO (DZOOK-kae-roh) *It.* Sugar.

ZUPPA (DZOOP-pah) *It.* Soup.

ZUPPA DI VONGOLE (dee VOHN-goh-lae) A Neapolitan specialty; literally, clam soup. What this turns out to be, though, is really steamed clams in their shells, in a sauce. The sauce is made of chopped tomatoes, olive oil, garlic, chopped parsley, and grated pepper, sometimes also small red peppers. This is served over, or with, slices of toast.

ZUPPA INGLESE See Inglese, Zuppa.

ZUPPA PAVESE See Pavese, Zuppa.

On the Cheese Tray

ANFROM, *Cn.* A lesser version of Oka.

APPENZELL (AHP-pen-tsel) *Sw.* Appenzell has a wrinkled brownish skin (edible) and a deep yellow interior dotted with small holes. It has a firm texture. The flavor ranges from somewhat fruity to very fruity, depending on its age. Appenzell has a more pronounced flavor than Gruyère or Emmental. Originally made in the eastern Swiss Canton of Appenzell, this cow's-milk cheese has been known since the time of Charlemagne (742-814).

APPENZELL RAES (AHP-pen-tsel raez) *Sw.* This cheese, a product of skimmed (cow's) milk, is steeped in wine for several weeks or longer. The result is a sharp (raes) pungent Appenzell of a grayish color.

ASAGIO (ah-SAH-joh) *It.* This cow's-milk cheese has a dark inedible rind, a granular texture, and a flavor which is somewhat sharp. Asagio is often used for grating. It is named for the area where it was first made in about 1870.

BABYBEL, *Fr.* This well-known cow's-milk cheese with the bright red paraffin covering is semi-soft and mild-tasting. Similar to Edam.

BAGNES (BA-nyu) *Sw.* Sometimes called Raclette, this cow's-milk cheese is from the Bagnes Valley of Switzerland. Being a good melter, it is perhaps best known for its role in the melted-cheese dish called Raclette. It has a slightly rough, inedible rind. Its

133

texture is firm, but with some elasticity. Bagnes is an aromatic cheese with a fruity flavor.

BANON (ba-NAWɴ) *Fr.* Banon is made in Provence from cow's, sheep's, or goat's milk, generally the latter. This soft ripened cheese is covered with herbs such as savory and/or wrapped in grape or chestnut leaves. It is dipped in eau *de vie de marc,* and placed in stone jars to ripen. Pale yellow in color, with a strong, tart flavor, Banon is small, flat, and round in shape.

BEAUFORT (boh-FAWR) *Fr.* This Gruyère-type cheese made from cow's milk is produced in Savoie. It has a firm, supple texture with irregular cracks. Beaufort is light and fragrant, and a good melter.

BEAUMONT (boh-MAWɴ) *Fr.* A cow's-milk cheese from the Haute Savoie, Beaumont is related to Saint-Paulin and other monastery-type cheeses. It is covered with a bright yellow rind, and has a delicate, supple texture. As it ages, its relatively mild flavor acquires a stronger taste.

BEL PAESE (bael pah-AE-zae) *It.* A name for Italy used by both Dante and Petrarch, literally, beautiful land. Bel Paese is the brand name of a group of cow's-milk cheeses. Although Bel Paese was first made commercially around 1920, this type of cheese has been known in Italy since about the turn of this century. Each package of Bel Paese bears a map of Italy, giving prominence to the little town of Melzo (near Milan) where Bel Paese was originally made. The domestic imitation is deceptively labeled with a map also, of North America, which at a glance has passed for the original. Bel Paese, made from fresh whole milk, is ivory white in color with a soft texture that is yielding to the touch. It is fast ripening with a mild, fruity flavor. It is also an excellent melter. Saint-Paulin is a similar cheese.

BIERKÄSE (BEER-kae-ze) *Gm.* Bierkäse reputedly derived its name, "beer cheese," from the practice of dissolving it in a stein of beer and drinking cheese and beer down together *(Ein, Zwei, G'saufer!)*. Enthusiasts claim it's better than an egg in your beer. This small, round, white cheese is somewhat strong in flavor. It is similar to an aged Brick. Bierkäse, a Bavarian cow's-milk cheese, is sometimes called Weisslacker, "white lacquer."

BLARNEY, *Ir.* Blarney is a mild, Swiss-style cheese made from cow's milk. Inside its bright red wax covering is a butter-yellow cheese with numerous small eyes, or holes.

BLEU OR BLUE CHEESE (bluh) There are over fifty varieties of blue cheese, all having a somewhat sharp and savory flavor. An internal mold (beneficial, of course) causes the blue veining or marbling. The best known and most highly regarded of these marbled cheeses are Roquefort (France), the oldest; Gorgonzola (Italy) and Stilton (England), which see. There are many others, from a number of other countries as well

BONBEL (bawn-BEL) *Fr* This is the brand name for a small, round commercial Saint-Paulin cheese. It is encased in a bright yellow paraffin covering. Bonbel is a semi-soft cow's-milk cheese with a very mild flavor and a slight sour tang.

BOURSAULT (boor-SOH) *Fr.* Boursault is the brand name for a triple crème cheese made in Normandy and Ile-de-France from cow's milk. Tender and very creamy, it has a mild flavor, with a delicate, nutty taste. The rind is a downy white.

BOURSIN (boor-SAN) *Fr.* This is the brand name of a creamy, rich triple crème cheese made in Normandy and Ile-de-France from cow's milk. Boursin comes either natural or flavored (with garlic and herbs, or pepper).

BRICK, *U.S.A.* First made in the mid-nineteenth century by a Wisconsin dairyman of Swiss descent, Brick gets its name from the object which the cheesemaker pressed onto the curd to force out the whey. Brick, also shaped like its namesake, is medium yellow to orange in color, with many small irregular holes. When young, this semi-soft cheese is sweet and mild, but develops pungent overtones that sharpen with age.

BRIE (bree) *Fr.* More words of praise have been sung about this cheese than any other. And perhaps more tears of disappointment shed as well, for it is uncommon to find one in perfect condition in this country. Brie is a round, flat disk made in four sizes: 13, 16, 22, and 4.5 inches in diameter. It is covered with an edible downy white rind that at times appears to be sprinkled with reddish pigment. The interior is a light, shiny yellow. When fully ripe, Brie should be soft and bulging, but not runny. Its texture should be the same throughout— supple, with no powdery section in the center. (That pale, powdery section sometimes lurking in the center of your Brie, which may be hidden even in a wedge by the cheese bulging above and below like the letter B, is a sign of stunted growth. Having been cut up before it was ripe, it will never ripen properly). This downy rind cheese has a fruity flavor and a pronounced tang. Some tasters note a faint aroma of mushrooms. An overripe Brie will have an odor of ammonia—a sure sign that a cheese has gone past the point of no return. Three of the better-known Bries are Brie de Meaux, Brie de Coulommiers, and Brie de Melun. The first is the

136

best, but the last is more common in the United States. Brie de Coulommiers often has had a little cream added to it. A single Brie requires fourteen to twenty-two quarts of (cow's) milk, according to size (not counting the 4.5-inch baby Bries). The season for Brie is November to May, but it is at its best from December to March.

BRILLAT-SAVARIN (bree-YA sa-va-RAn) *Fr.* This triple crème cheese from Normandy is named for Jean Anthelme Brillat-Savarin, author of *La Physiologie du goût* and a gastronome of note. Brillat-Savarin (the cheese, now) is covered with a downy, white rind. This small (5 x 1½ inch) soft cow's-milk cheese has a rich flavor hinting of slightly sour milk. Similar to Boursault.

CABECOU (ka-be-KOO) *Fr.* A soft, mild, nutty-flavored cheese with a smooth bluish rind, Cabecou is made from the milk of sheep or goats. "Cabecou" is the contraction of a Langue d'Oc word meaning "little goat."

CACIOCAVALLO (kah-choh-kah-VAHL-loh) *It.* Literally, cheese on horseback. This is a Provolone-type cheese, but with less butterfat. It is generally shaped sort of like a pear or gourd, but also comes in other shapes. Two cheeses are often tied together with a cord. Covered with an inedible glossy exterior crust, Caciocavallo has a hard, smooth, white interior. It is made from skimmed cow's milk. Caciocavallo has a mild, smoky flavor—it is often, but not always, smoked. Good eating when young, it becomes good for cooking as well as it ages. Why "on horseback"? Well, there are a few theories. One has it that the cheese was originally made from mare's milk. This cheese *is* believed to have been brought to Italy by the barbarian hordes. And, as we all know, Attila and the boys drank mare's milk. Another explanation tells us that the name comes from the practice of tying two cheeses together with a cord, very convenient for carrying on horseback— just drape them over the horse's neck. And then again, there's the theory that the name is derived from the seal of the Kingdom of Naples, a galloping horse, which used to be stamped on the cheese. Take your pick—we're rather taken with the mare's-milk theory ourselves.

CAERPHILLY (kahr-FIH-lu) *Wl.* This is a flat, circular cheese, weighing about 10 pounds, with a 9-inch diameter and a thickness of 2½ to 3½ inches. It is supposed to be a favorite with the Welsh miners. Caerphilly, named for the town where it was first made, in Glamorganshire, Wales, is snowy white in color, with a mild, slightly salty buttermilk flavor. This saltiness comes from the brine it is steeped in. It is made from cow's milk. The texture is semi-soft and granular; when broken, it is crumbly. Cheshire is a fair substitute.

CAMEMBERT (ka-mahn-BAER) *Fr.* This semi-soft cheese, known for centuries, is reputed to have been created in 1791 by Mme. Marie Harel of Camembert in Normandy. A small, round (4½ inches in diameter, 1½ inches thick) cow's-milk cheese, it is in season from October to June, and at its best from January to April. The surface of Camembert is covered with an edible downy white rind flecked with red. The interior is pale yellow; the texture supple and yielding to the touch. The flavor of Camembert is distinctive and pronounced—similar to that of Brie or Coulommiers.

CANTAL (kan-TAL) *Fr.* Cantal is a hard, smooth, golden cheese with a mild, nutty flavor. It comes in the shape of a tall cylinder (14 to 18 inches in diameter, 14 to 16 inches high) weighing up to 100 pounds. This cheese is made from cow's milk in the Cantal Mountains of the Auvergne. Pliny the Elder had praise for the cheese of Cantal. It is used as a table cheese and in cooking.

CAPRICE DES DIEUX (ka-PREES dae DYUH) *Fr.* Literally, caprice, or whim, of the gods. This little (7-ounce) cheese produced in the Haute Marne district from cow's milk is made in an oval shape. It is covered with an edible white downy rind. Caprice des Dieux is a semi-soft double crème cheese, mild in flavor.

CAPRINO ROMANO, *It.* See Romano.

CARRÉ DE L'EST (ka-RAE duh LEST) *Fr.* Literally, square of the east. This is a square-shaped cow's-milk cheese (3¾ inches across) with a downy white exterior and a pale yellow interior. And it comes from the east too, if Champagne, Alsace, or Lorraine happens to be east of where you are. Supple to the touch, milky to the taste, with a slight mushroom aroma, Carré de l'Est is similar to Camembert.

CARRÉ DEMI-SEL (ka-RAE du-mee SEL) *Fr.* This little cheese is just what its name says. It's a soft, double crème cheese, mild in flavor and slightly salty (demi-sel). It is small and square (carré) in shape.

CHABICHOU (sha-bee-SHOO) *Fr.* This cheese from the Poitou district is shaped like a small cylinder, and covered with an edible blue-gray rind. It is a soft goat cheese with a pronounced flavor that sharpens with age.

CHAOURCE (sha-OORS) *Fr.* This soft, downy white rind cheese is made in the Champagne district of France from cow's milk. Similar to Camembert, although larger in size, it is rich and creamy in flavor.

CHEDDAR, AMERICAN The first cheese factory

in the United States was established by Jesse Williams near Rome, New York, in 1851 to make Cheddar. Today the most notable American Cheddars come from New York, Vermont, and Wisconsin. New York Cheddar runs the gamut from the mildly sharps to those with pronounced sharpness. Vermont Cheddars are tangy and sharp. Wisconsin Cheddars range from very mild to sharp. Color these domestic versions nearly white to pale orange; which is, by the way, no indication of the degree of sharpness—it all depends on who's making it.

CHEDDAR, CANADIAN Canadian Cheddar is similar to the Cheddar of its neighbor to the south, and has been made in Canada for nearly as long—since 1864, when the first cheese factory founded by Harvey Farrington opened its doors in Ontario.

CHEDDAR, ENGLISH Cheddar cheese was first made in the latter part of the sixteenth century, in the Cheddar district of Somersetshire. This pressed cheese has a firm, crumbly texture and a pronounced, slightly sharp flavor. Cheddar comes in all sizes—Queen Victoria was presented with a 1,232-pounder. Oh, they don't make them like they used to. We should expect to find them much smaller than that. Other English cheeses similar to Cheddar are Cheshire, Gloucester, and Leicester.

CHESHIRE (CHE-sher, CHE-sheer) *Br.* Cheshire is produced in the village of Chester—which may explain why this cheese is called Chester in France. This pressed cheese is milder and less firm than Cheddar, and has a moist, crumbly texture that is also less compact. Its flavor is pronounced and sharp. It is made from cow's milk. Cheshire, first made some five hundred years earlier than Cheddar (placing it in the eleventh century), may be the oldest cheese of England—it is the oldest to which reference can be found. The special qualities of this cheese are attributed to the rich salt deposits found in the soil of Chester (which flavor the grass, which flavors the milk, which flavors the cheese that Chester makes). Cheshire comes in three colors: red, white, and blue. The most common, the red, derives its color from annatto—salmon-red-colored seeds from the fruit of a South American evergreen tree. (Annatto is a common coloring agent.) The white Cheshire is actually pale yellow. The blue is rich and has a unique flavor. An old blue Cheshire, quite rare, is a mature red with blue veining. Could it have been the flavor of this cheese that the Cheshire cat was grinning about?

CHESTER (ches-TER) *Fr.* Chester is a slightly sharp cow's-milk cheese with a pronounced flavor. It is similar to English Cheshire and Cheddar.

CHÈVRE (shevr) *Fr.* Chèvre is the generic name for young, relatively fresh, goat's-milk cheeses. These cheeses, of which there are some seventy-five varieties in France alone, have a pronounced, somewhat sourish flavor.

CHEVROTIN (shu-vraw-TAɴ) *Fr.* A goat's-milk cheese made in the shape of a truncated cone. It is soft and creamy with a somewhat nutty flavor. The flavor gets stronger with age.

CHRISTIAN IX, *Dn.* See King Christian.

COLBY, *U.S.A.* Colby is a light yellow cow's-milk cheese similar to a mild Cheddar, but softer and moister. It is named for Colby Township, Wisconsin, where it was first made in 1882.

COMTÉ (kawn-TAE) *Fr.* Comté ranges from mild to somewhat sharp in flavor. This cow's-milk cheese, known since the thirteenth century, is very similar to Gruyère.

CONCHES (kawnsh) *Sw.* This cheese, also known as

Raclette, is made in the Conches Valley of Switzerland. It is similar to Bagnes, which see.

COON, *U.S.A.* Coon, another Cheddar-type cheese, is orange-yellow in color with an inedible black rind and a crumbly texture. It is sharp and tangy. Coon is cured by a special patented method.

COULOMMIERS (koo-lawm-YAE) *Fr.* A soft cheese covered with a downy white edible rind, it is similar to Brie de Meaux—at least to the one found in the United States. As found here, it is in season from November to April and is best avoided in the summer. In the Brie district of Coulommiers this cheese is usually eaten, after salting, when it is fresh—before the white mold covers its surface. It is made from cow's milk.

COTTAGE CHEESE Cottage cheese, made from skimmed milk, is a soft, uncured cheese with a fresh milk flavor. It is a cow's-milk cheese, delicate in taste and aroma although slightly acid. Cottage cheese is low in butterfat and high in protein and calcium. Whipped cream cottage cheese has had whipped cream added to the cottage cheese. Cottage cheese is also made as a pot cheese, from buttermilk and soured milk, or yogurt, drained and pressed in a pot.

CREAM CHEESE Cream cheese is the mildest form of cheese. Made from milk and cream, cream cheese has a light texture and a soft, mild, creamy flavor. This white cheese is often used as a spread.

DANABLU (DAH-nah-bloo) *Dn.* This Danish blue cheese is semi-soft, and ivory-colored with a marbling of blue-green mold. It is a cow's-milk cheese with a rich, spicy, rather sharp flavor.

DANBO (DAHN-boh) *Dn.* This cow's-milk cheese, at one time known as Danish Steppe, is firm to hard in texture, with an inedible rind and a square shape. It is pale gold in color and has a mild, tangy flavor. Danbo is sometimes spiced with caraway seeds.

DERBY (DAHR-bee) *Br.* Derby cheese is named after Derbyshire, where it is produced. Similar to Cheddar, another English cow's-milk cheese, Derby is more crumbly, and moist; it also ripens sooner.

DOUBLE CRÈME (doobl krem) *Fr.* Double crème cheeses are rich, creamy, soft cheeses containing 60 to 74 percent butterfat. Sometimes flavored, they are generally sold under a brand name.

DOUBLE GLOUCESTER (dubl GLAW-ster) *Br.* Pale orange in color, this cow's-milk cheese is milder and less crumbly than Cheddar. It is firm-textured, mild yet rich, and with a slight sharpness. There is also a single Gloucester (less aged) but it is rarely seen in the United States. This cheese is named for Gloucestershire in the west of England, where it is made.

DUNLOP, *Sc.* This is another Cheddar-style cheese. It is covered with an inedible black rind, and the interior ranges in color from white to deep cream. Dunlop is a cow's-milk cheese with a somewhat sweetish flavor, but with a slight sharpness. It is a good melter. Older cheeses are used for grating. Dunlop is named for the little town of Dunlop in Ayrshire in the southwest part of Scotland, where it was first made by Barbara Gilmour in 1688.

EDAM (ae-DAHM) *Hl.* This spherical cheese is encased in a red or yellow inedible (paraffin) covering. It is semi-hard with a supple texture. Light yellow, smooth, and mellow with a mild, nutty flavor, Edam is made in northern Holland from partly skimmed (cow's) milk, and is named for a small town near Amsterdam. Edam has been made since the Middle Ages. Gouda is a very similar cheese.

ELBO, *Dn.* This oblong cow's-milk cheese with the reddish brown rind is similar to, but milder than Samsøe, another Danish cheese.

EMMENTAL, EMMENTHAL (EM-men-tahl) *Sw.* Emmental is named for the Emme Valley (tal) in the Canton of Bern, where it has been made since the sixteenth century. This cheese, often called Swiss cheese, is famous for the parts that aren't there—the holes. Light yellow in color, firm-textured with large spherical holes, Emmental is nutlike and buttery. Some wheels of Emmental weigh over 200 pounds, requiring over a ton of cow's-milk to make. Emmental wasn't always so big; in the beginning it was much smaller. But it seems that when the cheeses were taken to market they went through a toll station and were taxed—by the piece, regardless of the size. It didn't take long before the cheeses of Emmental began to grow, and grow, until they became the giant wheels we see today. Emmental is now also made in much smaller (about 25-pound) loaves as well. It is used as a table cheese and in cooking.

ESROM (ES-rawm) *Dn.* This cow's-milk cheese is almost white in color, soft and pliant to the touch, and dotted with small holes. Esrom, named for the town where it's made, is mild to medium flavored, very similar to Port Salut.

FARMER'S CHEESE Farmer's cheese is closely related to pot (cottage) cheese. It is white in color, mild, and slightly sour in flavor. It is firmer, and less moist, than cottage cheese.

FÉTA (FAE-tah) *Gr.* Féta cheese is made from sheep's

milk, sometimes also cow's and goat's milk. It is a soft, white, crumbly cheese, salty, and with a distinctive, somewhat acid flavor. The saltiness comes from the brine it is pickled in. Féta is used in cooking, eaten fresh as a table cheese and in Greek salad.

FONDU AU MARC DU RAISIN (fawn-DEW oh mar dew rae-ZAɴ) *Fr.* This processed cheese ("fondu" means melted) from the Savoie is covered with grape skins and seeds ("marc" is the dregs, or residue, of winemaking). It is small, flat, and round. The cheese, made from cow's milk, is white in color, with a buttery texture and a mild flavor. The crust of seeds is not recommended for eating.

FONTAINEBLEU (fawn-taen-BLUH) *Fr.* Fontainebleu is a light, creamy, fresh cheese made from cow's milk mixed with whipped cream.

FONTINA (fohn-TEE-nah) *It.* This cheese has been made in the Aosta Valley, high up in the mountains of northwestern Italy, since the eleventh century. It was originally a sheep's-milk cheese, but is now made from cow's milk. Covered with a light brownish rind, Fontina's interior color ranges from ivory to yellow. Its firm, supple texture is dotted with very small eyes. It is delicate in flavor with a nutty sweetness, somewhat similar to Emmental, but with a slight tang, like Gruyère. As Fontina matures, its flavor sharpens. This cheese, a superb melter, is the cheese used in Fonduta; it's a fine table cheese as well.

FROMAGE DE PYRÉNÉES (fraw-MAHZH duh pih-re-NE) *Fr.* See Tomme de Pyrénées.

FRIULANA (free-oo-LAH-nah) *It.* Friulana, from the northeastern corner of Italy (Friuli), is yellow in color and firm in texture. It has a mild flavor with a piquant touch.

145

FYNBO (FEWN-boh) *Dn.* Fynbo comes in 7- to 8-ounce rounds covered with an inedible rind. This semi-soft pale yellow cow's-milk cheese, mild in flavor, is named for the island of Fünen or Fyn, in southern Denmark where it is made (and which incidentally, was Hans Christian Andersen's home).

GAMMELOST (GAHM-mel-ohst) *Nr.* This is a semi-soft, blue-veined cheese made from sour milk, which may account for the name ("gammel" means old), referring to the condition of the milk, not of the cheese, which is eaten young, not aged. This cylindrical, cow's-milk cheese has a crumbly texture and is somewhat sharp and aromatic.

GERVAIS (zhaer-VAE) *Fr.* Gervais is the brand name of a Petit-Suisse, a soft, fresh, double crème cow's-milk cheese.

GJETOST (YAE-tohst) *Nr.* Gjetost has been the national cheese of Norway for over one hundred years. The name means goat cheese. At one time this firm, unripened, brown-colored cheese was made entirely from goat's milk, but today it is the product of 90 percent cow's milk and 10 percent goat's milk. Gjetost has a sweetish, caramel-like flavor.

GLARNERKÄSE (GLAHR-ner-kae-ze) *Sw.* Literally, the cheese of Glarus. See Sapsago.

GOAT'S-MILK CHEESE See Chèvre.

GORGONZOLA (gohr-gohn-TSOH-lah) *It.* Gorgonzola, produced in the Po Valley since the ninth century, is one of the triumvirate of great blues, the others being Roquefort and Stilton. Semi-soft and creamy, this yellowish white, or cream-colored cheese marbled with green mold is the softest and creamiest of the veined cheeses. It is savory to almost sharp in flavor, and has a strong bouquet. Gorgonzola is named for the village not far from Milan where it was first produced, a halting place for the herds of cows being driven from summer pastures in the mountains down to the plains. They were milked here and the overflow was made into cheese. Gorgonzola as we know it, though, is believed to be an accidental creation. Apparently there was such an abundant supply of cheese after one of these rest stops by the herds that some of it was not eaten until it had sat in storage for some time, developing those veins of green mold for which it has since become famous. The cheeses used to be aged in the natural caves of the Valsassina, and some still may be, but mostly now they develop in the storerooms of the cheese companies.

GOUDA (GOW-dah) *Hl.* Gouda, named for the Dutch town, is made in the southern part of the country. It has a smooth yellow rind covered with yellow wax. It is firm, yet supple, to the touch. Made from whole cow's milk, Gouda has a mild, nutlike flavor that improves with age. Edam is a very similar cheese.

GOURMANDISE (goor-mahn-DEEZ) *Fr.* Gourmandise is a double crème cheese that has been melted (processed) and often flavored, most commonly with kirsch (cherry) or walnuts. The name, believe it or not, means gluttony.

GRÄDDOST (GRAHD-oost) *Sw.* This is a semi-soft, double-rich cow's-milk cheese from Sweden. It is pale yellow with irregular eyes, and has a mild, sweet flavor. "Grädde" is the Swedish word for cream.

GRANA (GRAH-nah) *It.* Grana is the generic name for the granular-textured (hence the name) grating

147

cheeses of which Parmigiano (Parmesan) is the most highly regarded. These yellow cheeses have a hard but somewhat crumbly, grainy texture, and a piquant flavor and aroma. In the U.S.A. two types of Italian cheeses are called Parmesan. Real Parmesan (Parmigiano Reggiano) must come from a strictly delimited zone and be at least two years old before it is sold. Additionally, it can be made only from mid-April to November 11. Parmigiano is made from cow's milk of uniform quality, while the milk used to make Grana Padano (known since the thirteenth century) varies in quality. Padano is from one to two years old when it is sold. It is produced year-round throughout northern Italy.

GREYERZER (grae-YAER-tser) *Sw.* The German name for Gruyère, which see.

GRÜNERKÄSE, GRÜNERKRAUTERKÄSE (GREW-ner-kae-ze, GREW-ner-krow-ter-kae-ze) *Sw.* Literally, green cheese, and green herb cheese. See Sapsago.

GRUYÈRE (grew-YAER) *Sw.* Gruyère has been made since at least the twelfth century in the Gruyères Valley of the Jura mountains in the canton of Fribourg. It is a firm-textured cow's-milk cheese ranging in color from ivory to light amber. It is covered with an inedible wrinkled brown rind. Like the similar but blander Emmental, Gruyère is dotted with holes—but they are much smaller and fewer. Its flavor is sweet and nutlike. Gruyère grates quite well, and is often used in cooking. French Gruyère is similar to, but tangier and less sweet than, the Swiss original.

HAND CHEESE, *U.S.A.* Hand cheese is a sour-milk cheese made from cow's milk. It is a small flat oval cheese, originally shaped by hand. Hand cheese has a pungent aroma and strong flavor. It is sometimes flavored with caraway seeds.

HANDKÄSE (HAHNT-kae-ze) *Gm.* This cheese, originally shaped by hand, at home (the name means hand cheese), is a sour-milk cheese made from cow's milk. It is soft to medium firm in texture, with a yellow interior and an orange to reddish brown rind. Handkäse has a strong aroma and a strong, pungent flavor. It is sometimes flavored with caraway seeds. Also called Harzer or Harzerkäse.

HARVARTI (hahr-VAHR-tee) *Dn.* Harvarti, a cow's-milk cheese, ranges from semi-soft to firm in texture. It is pale yellow with large to small eyes (holes). When young it is mild, bland, and slightly sweet-tasting; as it ages, its flavor sharpens. It is similar to Tilsit. Harvarti was first made by Hanne Nielsen, who had traveled abroad to learn about cheesemaking and returned home to experiment with many types. The cheese is named after her farm, Harvarthi.

HARZER, HARZERKÄSE (HAHRT-tser-kae-ze) *Gm.* Handkäse from the Harzer Mountains. See Handkäse.

HERKIMER, *U.S.A.* Herkimer is a fairly dry, crumbly-textured, sharp Cheddar-type cheese from New York State. It is pale in color, nearly white. It is named after Herkimer county, where it was first made.

HERRGÅRD, HERRGÅRDOST (HAER-gawrd, HAER-gawrd-oost) *Sd.* Herrgård is a cow's-milk cheese with small eyes and a nutlike flavor. It may be semi-firm or hard. The half-cream type is similar to Gouda; the full-cream type like Emmental. The name Herrgårdost means "manor cheese." It was originally made on the farms of western Sweden.

JACK, *U.S.A.* See Monterey Jack

JARLSBERG (YAHRLS-berg) *Nr.* Jarlsberg is a wide-eyed, firm, smooth-textured cow's-milk cheese. It has a buttery, nutlike flavor. It is very similar to Emmental in appearance and taste. It was named for an old estate on the Oslo fjord where cheesemaking in Norway supposedly got its start.

KASHKAVAL, KASKAVAL (kash-kah-vahl) Kashkaval is a cylindrical, granular-textured, elastic cheese made throughout the Balkans from partly skimmed sheep's milk. It has an inedible amber-colored rind; the interior is yellow and has a few holes. Kaskaval has a mildly sharp, piquant flavor and aroma.

KASSERI (kahs-sae-ree) *Gr.* Kasseri is a semi-soft to firm white cheese made from goat's or sheep's milk. It has an edible rind, a crumbly texture, and a strong flavor and aroma. It is used as a table cheese when fresh, a grating cheese when dried.

KING CHRISTIAN IX, *Dn.* This cheese, named after the nineteenth-century Danish king, is a mild, Samsøe-type cheese flavored with caraway seeds. The seeds impart a strong flavor to the cheese as it ages; consequently, the younger this cheese is, the better.

KRAUTERKÄSE (KROW-ter-kae-ze) *Sw.* Literally, herb cheese. See Sapsago.

LANCASHIRE (LANG-ku-sher, LANG-ku-sheer) *Br.* Lancashire is a creamy, white Cheddar-type cheese, but softer, moister, crumblier, stronger, and more flavorful than either Cheddar or Cheshire. It is the softest of the hard, pressed cheeses. A good melter, from the Fylde district of Lancashire.

LAPPI (LAP-pee) *Fn.* Lappi is a semi-hard yet supple Finnish cow's-milk cheese with a mild flavor. It is pale yellow to yellowish orange in color.

LEICESTER, LEICESTERSHIRE (LES-ter, LES-ter-sher, LES-ter-sheer) *Br.* Leicestershire is another Cheddar-style cheese. This one is bright yellow to orange or light red (colored with natural annatto dye). It is rich in flavor with a slight tang. Leicester has a loose, flaky texture and is moister and more crumbly than Cheddar or Cheshire. It melts well.

LEIDEN (LII.-dun) *Hl.* See Leyden.

LEVROUX (lu-VROO) *Fr.* Levroux is a pyramid-shaped soft goat's-milk cheese from the district of Berry. Named for the fortified town of Levroux in the neighborhood of where the cheese is made.

LEYDEN (LII-dun) *Hl.* Leyden is a mild, aromatic, caraway-flavored cheese. It is semi-soft to firm, and pale yellow in color. Leyden is made from partly skimmed (cow's) milk and buttermilk. It is covered with a smooth, grayish, inedible rind.

LIEDERKRANZ (LEE-der-krants) *U.S.A.* This cheese was first made by Emil Frey in Monroe, New York, in 1878, in an attempt to copy the Belgian Limburger. Small and oblong in shape, weighing 4 ounces, this soft, moist cow's-milk cheese is covered with an edible light orange rind. The interior is a deep glossy yellow. Liederkranz is similar to, but less smelly and strong than, Limburger. The name (a brand name) is German for a collection of songs. Why songs? Well, if you are a fan of this cheese, you might sing its praises.

LIMBURGER (LIHM-buhr-ger) *Bl., Gm.* Limburger is known for its powerful smell and spicy, hearty, somewhat salty flavor. It is a cow's-milk cheese, semi-soft, and supple to the touch. Its smooth yellow interior is covered with an edible brick-red rind. Limburger is generally thought of as a German cheese, but it was first made in Belgium, in what was then the duchy of Limburg, later in Holland, and then finally in Germany. This cheese, like some others, is believed to have been created in one of the many monasteries in this area in the Middle Ages.

LIVAROT (lee-va-ROH) *Fr.* This cheese is known for its powerful, pungent aroma and strong, spicy flavor. The inedible glossy rind ranges in color from terra-cotta to deep chestnut; its interior is brownish yellow. Livarot, one of the most ancient cheeses of Normandy, is named for the nearest market town to its place of origin. It is believed to have been invented by monks, who like their brothers in many other monasteries were looking for something tasty to eat on their many fast days. Livarot comes in small discs (4½ to 5 inches in diameter, 1½ to 2 inches thick) weighing from 12 ounces to just over a pound. This soft, mold-ripened cow's-milk cheese is similar to, but stronger than, Pont L'Évêque.

LIVROUX (lee-VROO) *Fr.* See Levroux.

LONGHORN, *U.S.A.* This is a firm, yellowish orange, Cheddar-type cheese with a tangy flavor. It is supposed to be named for its similarity to the horns of longhorn cattle; it must be the color—it's not the shape.

LUCULLUS (loo-KOOL-us) *Fr.* Lucullus is a small (3 x 2 inch, 8-ounce) triple crème, with a downy pinkish rind and a mild, nutty flavor. Named presumably for Lucius Licinius Lucullus, Roman general and epicure.

MASCARPONE, MASCHERPONE (mah-skahr-POH-nae, mah-skaer-POH-nae) *It.* Mascarpone is a dessert cheese, served mixed with fruit and sugar, and sometimes sweet liqueurs. It is made from fresh cream, and has a buttery yellow color and a flavor quite similar to that of whipped cream.

MIMOLETTE FRANÇAIS (mee-moh-LET frahn-SAE) *Fr.* Mimolette Français, covered with a light gray inedible rind, is shaped like a slightly flattened sphere (8 inches in diameter, 7 inches high). It has a firm texture and an orange-yellow color. The flavor is somewhat nutty. This cow's-milk cheese, which is believed to have been introduced from Holland, is similar to Edam and Gouda.

MONDSEER SCHACHTELKÄSE (MOHNT-sae-er SHAHK-tel-kae-ze) *Au.* This cow's-milk cheese has a sharpish flavor, somewhat like a mild Limburger. Made in the shape of a small disc, it used to be shipped in wooden containers—Schackteln. From the Mondsee district of Austria.

MONTEREY JACK, *U.S.A.* Sometimes called Monterey or Jack, this is a Cheddar-style cheese, softer and more delicate, though, than Cheddar. It is semi-soft, and bland in flavor, although it increases in sharpness as it matures. The cheese is so called because it was first made, presumably from an old monks' recipe, in Monterey County, California, in 1892.

MONTRACHET (mawn-ra-SHAE) *Fr.* Montrachet is a supple, mild, creamy goat's-milk cheese made in Burgundy. Underneath the wrapping of chestnut or grape leaves, it is bluish in color. This log-shaped cheese is sometimes dusted with vine wood ash.

MOZZARELLA (moh-tsah-REL-lah) *It.* This cheese, originally made from buffalo milk, is now mainly a cow's-milk cheese, though sometimes it is a combination of the two. Mozzarella is snow white in color with a soft, somewhat elastic texture, and is

sold in salted and unsalted versions, the salt being
added by floating the cheese in salted water. Its
flavor is delicate and mild. When fresh, Mozzarella,
dripping in its own whey, has a sweet, milky
freshness. It is available in a variety of shapes,
being molded by hand while it is pliable into balls,
fat sacks, and braided ("trecce") shapes. A creamy
butterball Mozzarella is also made, as well as a tan-
colored smoky variety. Mozzarella is used as a table
cheese or in cooking (which heightens its flavor),
especially on pizza.

MÜNSTER (MEWN-ster) *Fr.* Münster, a cow's-milk
cheese from the Alsatian town of the same name, is
semi-soft and supple to the touch. It has a strong
smell and a strong, spicy flavor. Münster is covered
with an inedible, smooth, shiny brick-red rind, and
has a whitish yellow interior. This is an ancient
cheese, known since the Middle Ages. It is said that
monks from Ireland made the first Münster in the
Vosges of Alsace in the seventh century.

MYSOST (MEWS-ohst) *Nr.* Mysost is a whey cheese
similar to Gjetost. It is made from goat's or cow's
milk, or a combination of the two. It is light brown
in color with a buttery consistency and a mild,
sweetish flavor. "Myse" is Norwegian for whey,
"ost" for cheese.

NEC PLUS ULTRA (nek ploos OOL-trah) *Fr.*
Literally, no more beyond, the highest degree. A
processed cheese, like Gourmandise, and also walnut or cherry flavored.

NEUFCHÂTEL (nuh-shah-TEL) *Fr.* Neufchâtel is a
small (4-ounce), square, cylindrical, or heart-
shaped cheese covered with an edible downy white
rind sparsely flecked with red. Soft and mild, with
a smooth, velvety texture, Neufchâtel is savory and

somewhat salty in flavor. It is a cow's-milk cheese, and has a slight aroma of mold. Neufchâtel has been made in upper Normandy for a thousand years.

NØKKELOST (NAWK-kel-ohst) *Nr.* Nøkkelost is a semi-hard Gouda-type cheese made from cow's milk and seasoned with caraway, cumin, or cloves. The external coating surrounding the cheese is inedible. Because it melts well, it is often used in cooking.

NORBO (NAWR-boh) *Nr.* Norbo is a semi-firm, pale yellow cheese with a mild, nutlike flavor. It is covered with an inedible rind—wax, actually.

OKA (OH-kah) *Cn.* Made by Trappist monks at Oka, Quebec, this cheese resembles Camembert in appearance (8-ounce rounds), and in taste, Port Salut. The recipe for this cheese is supposed to have been smuggled out of France. Oka is a pale yellow or whitish yellow cheese covered with an edible crust. It is semi-hard and supple in texture. In flavor it ranges from mild to strong, depending on its age.

PARMIGIANO, PARMESAN (pahr-mee-JAH-noh) *It.* Parmigiano, or Parmesan, has been made in Italy for over nine hundred years in the area around Parma, Reggio-Emilia, Modena, Bologna, and Mantua. This cheese is without equal in the category of seasoning cheeses. It is grated over many dishes, but is also an excellent table cheese. It has a hard granular texture and a light yellow color. There is a slight sharpness to its distinctive flavor. Grana (which see), by comparison, is less grainy and less pronounced in flavor. Most cheese sold as Parmesan in the U.S.A. is in fact Grana (or a poor domestic imitation). (If required to limit ourselves to only one cheese for the rest of our lives, Parmigiano would undoubtedly be the cheese.)

PARMIGIANO-REGGIANO (raej-JAH-noh) *It.* The full name of Parmigiano, which see.

PECORINO (pae-koh-REE-noh) *It.* Pecorino is a snowy white, hard, compact, sheep's-milk cheese. It has a slightly smoky smell and a somewhat sharpish edge. Pecorino is the generic name for all Italian sheep's-milk cheeses, "pecora" being the Italian word for sheep, ewe. It is a very ancient cheese, mentioned by Pliny, and made in pre-Roman times. According to legend, Romulus, co-founder of Rome, made this cheese from a combination of sheep's and goat's milk.

PECORINO ROMANO   See Romano.

PECORINO DA TAVOLA (TAH-voh-lah) Pecorino da Tavola is a slightly pungent, firm table cheese ("tavola" is table) made from sheep's milk.

PEPATO (pae-PAH-toh) *It.* This is a spicy Pecorino (sheep's-milk) cheese made in Sicily and other parts of southern Italy. Pepato is spiced with pepper ("pepe").

PETIT-SUISSE (pu-tee SWEES) *Fr.* Petit-Suisse is a soft, unsalted double crème cheese made from fresh cow's milk, enriched with cream. It is small (1 x 2 inches, 1 ounce) and cylindrical in shape.

PONT-L'ÉVÊQUE (pawn-lae-VEK) *Fr.* This square (4-inch) cheese has an edible pale orange crust marked with indentations from the straw it has been set out on, and a pale yellow interior dotted with numerous small holes. Pont l'Évêque is plump and semi-soft to the touch, with a strong aromatic smell and a tangy flavor. This cheese is at its best in the autumn and winter. Pont l'Évêque (literally, bishop's bridge) has been made under this name since at least the thirteenth century in the Pays d'Auge in Normandy. It is named for the market town nearest to its place of origin.

PORT SALUT (pawr sa-LEW) *Fr.* Port Salut, yellow in color, is semi-soft, creamy, and relatively mild in flavor, although its flavor does become stronger with age. It is covered with an inedible orange rind. Saint-Paulin and Bel Paese are quite similar in style. This cow's-milk cheese was first made by Trappist monks in the nineteenth century, at the thirteenth-century monastery of Port du Salut (port of salvation) in Entrammes. Today, Port Salut, still made by the monks by a secret formula, is sold to a commercial firm that markets the cheese.

PROVOLONE (proh-voh-LOH-nae) *It.* Provolone comes in various sizes and shapes, some of them fanciful, like the little piglets occasionally seen in Italian delicatessens. This cheese is often hung like a little sack from a cord, sometimes by twos. The names it is sold under vary as well. Made from uncooked whole cow's milk, Provolone has a thin, smooth, inedible pale yellow crust, with a flaky texture, enclosing a creamy white interior. In flavor it ranges from mild to slightly sharp, often with a smoky taste and aroma, from having been smoked. The flavor sharpens with age. As it melts easily, it is often used in cooking. The young Provolone is generally used as a table cheese, while the browner, aged one is more often used for cooking and for grating. Originally made from buffalo milk, but now from cow's milk.

PYRAMIDE (pee-ra-MEED) *Fr.* See Valençay.

RACLETTE (ra-KLET) *Sw.* Raclette (from the French verb "racler," to scrape) is the name of a cheese dish of the Valais region. The cheeses that go into this dish, Bagnes and Conches, are often called Raclette cheese or simply Raclette.

REBLOCHON (ru-blaw-SHAWₙ) *Fr.* Reblochon has been made, from cow's milk, in the Haute Savoie for hundreds of years. The milk used is always from the second milking, never the first. It is round and flat with an edible yellowish pink rind and a semi-soft, creamy, buttery texture. The flavor is mild, creamy.

RICOTTA (ree-KOHT-tah) *It.* Ricotta is a white, creamy, bland cheese that was originally the by-product of other cheese, being made from the whey (although nowadays milk is added). It is similar to, but much smoother than, cottage cheese and without its acidity. When fresh, Ricotta is soft, moist, and creamy, verging on the sweet, with a mild nutlike flavor. As it ages and dries it becomes a table cheese, then a hard cheese suitable for grating. It is used in Lasagne, Ravioli, and Cannelloni, on pasta, and in many desserts.

RICOTTA SALATA (ree-KOHT-tah sah-LAH-tah) *It.* "Dried Ricotta" is firm, moist, and smooth. Its flavor is mild. It is pure white and without holes or eyes. Ricotta Salata is available in salted and unsalted versions, and is used both as a seasoning and as a table cheese.

ROMANO (roh-MAH-noh) *It.* Romano comes in several varieties. Pecorino (pae-koh-REE-noh) Romano is made from sheep's milk ("pecora" is ewe); Vacchino (vahk-KEE-noh) Romano is from cow's milk ("vacca" is cow); Caprino (kah-PREE-noh) Romano, from goat's milk ("capra" is goat). These cheeses are hard, compact, and granular. They are ivory colored, and range in flavor from mild to sharp, depending on their age. When young they are used as table cheese; when older, for grating.

ROQUEFORT (rohk-FAWR) *Fr.* Roquefort, made since at least the first century A.D., is the oldest of the blue-veined cheeses (it was mentioned by Pliny the Elder). Roquefort is made from ewe's milk and ripened in the huge natural caves of Cambalou above the town of Roquefort-sur-Soulzon. The milk may or may not be from sheep raised in the Aveyron Départment, but the cheese is made, impregnated with the special mold, and matured in the cold and humid chambers of the limestone caves there. Roquefort, considered by some the king of cheeses, has a white curd mottled with blue-green veining. Its texture is semi-soft and crumbly; its flavor, pungent, slightly salty, and somewhat sharp. Stilton, Gorgonzola, and Roquefort make up the triumvirate of great blues.

SAGE CHEESE, *U.S.A.* Sage cheese, made in Vermont, is a Cheddar-type cheese that has been spiced with sage.

SAGE DERBY (saej DAHR-bee) *Br.* This is Derby cheese that has been spiced by spreading chopped sage and sometimes spinach juice between layers of the curd. It is firm, with a pale green mottled color. This mild, sage-flavored cheese becomes stronger as it ages.

SAINT-NECTAIRE (san-nek-TAER) *Fr.* Saint-Nectaire, made in the Auvergne, and known since the time of Louis IV, is similar to Saint-Paulin. This cow's-milk cheese has a creamy texture and a mild tang. It is made in the shape of a flat disc and is covered with an inedible orange rind.

SAINT-PAULIN (san-paw-LAN) *Fr.* Saint-Paulin is a

tender, creamy-textured, and mild-flavored Port Salut-type cheese made from cow's milk.

SAINTE-MAURE (sant-MAWR) *Fr.* This is a goat's-milk cheese from Touraine. It is log-shaped, traditionally with a straw in the middle. Its flavor is mild when young, becoming stronger as it ages.

SAMSØE (SAM-suh) *Dn.* Samsøe is a buttery cow's-milk cheese with a firm texture, small eyes, and pale yellow color. It has a sweet, nutlike flavor that improves with age. It is very similar to Emmental, but softer, milder, and less distinctive than its Swiss counterpart. It is named for the island of Samsø, where it is made.

SAPSAGO (SAHP-sah-goh) *Sw.* Sapsago is a small, very hard, cow's-milk cheese, often used for grating. It is made from slightly soured skimmed milk and has a sharp, pungent flavor and an aromatic aroma. This cheese, flavored with powdered clover leaves or fenugreek, is light green in color. It is made in the form of a truncated cone. Sapsago has been made in the Swiss Canton of Glarus for over a thousand years, originally by monks (without the herbs). It is also called Schabziger, Schabzieger, Glarnerkäse, Grünerkäse, Krauterkäse, and Grünerkrauterkäse.

SARDO (SAHR-doh) *It.* Sardo is a Romano-type cheese from Sardinia (Sardegna). The name means Sardinian. Originally made from ewe's milk, it is now made from a mixture of ewe's and cow's milk. When mature, it is used for grating.

SBRINZ (sbrihnts) *Sw.* See Spalen.

SCAMORZE (skah-MOHR-tsae) *It.* Scamorze, from Abruzzi, was originally made only from buffalo milk; today cow's and/or goat's milk is also used. This oval or gourd-shaped cheese is semi-soft, smooth, and pliable (like Mozzarella). It is sometimes smoked (like Provolone), and has a slightly rancid smell and a mild, salty flavor. Scamorze is eaten fresh, or used for cooking. This cheese is a good melter.

SCHABZIEGER, SCHABZIGER (SHAHB-zee-ger, SHAHB-zih-ger) *Sw.* See Sapsago.

SPALEN (SPAH-len) *Sw.* Spalen is a hard cow's-milk cheese originally made in the canton of Unterwalden, now in other central Swiss cantons as well. Spalen is pale yellow in color, with a mildly sharp, nutty flavor. The fully cured Spalen, used for grating, is called Sbrinz. It is the Swiss answer to the Italian Grana. This cheese takes the name Spalen from the little wooden boxes it is shipped in.

STEPPE (STEP-pe) *Dn.* This cheese was first made by Germans living in Russia—on the steppes of Russia, no doubt. Better known as Danbo, which see.

STILTON *Br.* An inedible wrinkled melonlike rind covers this off-white cheese marbled with narrow blue-green veins of mold. Stilton is a double crème cow's-milk cheese, semi-soft with a firm, supple texture. It has a rich, piquant flavor that, although pronounced, is milder than that of Gorgonzola or Roquefort. Stilton is the perfect accompaniment to vintage Port. It has a tall cylindrical shape. Stilton is believed to have been first made in 1730 by Mrs. Orton of Little Dalby in Leicestershire, but to have acquired its name some years later when it was sold at a popular inn in Stilton.

STRACCHINO (strahk-KEE-noh) *It.* Stracchino is the generic name for the group of uncooked creamy white cheeses, made since 1100 from the milk of cows passing through the Lombardian plains on their way south for the winter. The cows are tired from their trek—"stracca" is the local dialect word for "tired." The milk from the morning milking is mixed with that from the previous evening's to produce Piccante (piquant) Stracchino. Dolce (sweet) Stracchino is the product of a single milking. The most famous variety of Stracchino is Gorgonzola.

SVECIA, SVECIAOST (SVE-syah, SVE-syah-oost) *Sd.* Svecia is a firm cow's-milk cheese similar to Gouda but more open-textured, with little irregular eyes. It is orange in color, with an inedible crust. Svecia is sometimes flavored with caraway seeds and cloves. The flavor ranges from mild to medium sharp.

SWISS CHEESE Swiss cheese generally means Emmental, or a domestic processed cheese that is a poor imitation of that great cheese.

TAFFELOST (TAHF-fel-ohst) *Nr.* This "table cheese" is a sharp-flavored whey cheese resembling Mysost. It is made in 6-pound loaves. Taffelost is firm and smooth-textured with eyes of various sizes.

TALEGGIO (tah-LAEJ-joh) *It.* Taleggio, produced in the Lombardian valley of the same name, is of recent origin, having been first made after World War I. This cheese comes in 8-inch squares, 2 inches thick, weighing 4 pounds. It is covered with a moldy crust which is inedible. Its texture is creamy and pastelike; the color, ivory white. It is a fast-ripening cheese, and its fresh, mellow taste sharpens with age. Taleggio is actually a soft, creamy Stracchino.

TILSIT, TILSITER (TIHL-siht, TIHL-siht-er) *Gm.* Tilsit is a medium firm, light yellow cheese dotted with many tiny holes. Its flavor ranges from mild to mildly sharp to piquant; it improves with age. Tilsit is similar to Harvarti (sometimes called

"Danish Tilsit"). This cow's-milk cheese was first made by Dutch immigrants who settled near Tilsit in East Prussia.

TOMME DE PYRÉNÉES (tawm duh pih-ra-NAE) *Fr.* This cheese, also known as Fromage de Pyrénées, is semi-soft and mild. An inedible black rind covers the exterior of this flat, round cheese.

TOMME DE SAVOIE (tawm duh sa-VWAH) *Fr.* This is a semi-soft, mold-ripened, cow's-milk cheese. It is ivory to yellow with a mild, slightly nutty flavor.

TRAPPIST CHEESE This name refers to a group of monastery cheeses of which Port Salut (see) is the most famous.

TRIPLE CRÈME (trihpl krem) *Fr.* Triple crème cheeses must contain 75 percent or more of butterfat. They are creamy and rich. Sometimes flavorings are added. These small, cylindrical cheeses when unflavored are covered with an edible white crust. They are often sold under a brand name.

TYBO (TEW-boh) *Dn.* Tybo is a brick-shaped semi-hard cheese from the district of Thy, sometimes made with caraway seeds. This hard cow's-milk cheese is covered with an inedible wax coating. It is aromatic and relatively mild, but its flavor sharpens as it ages.

VACCHINO ROMANO *It.* See Romano.

VALENÇAY (va-lahn-SAE) *Fr.* Valençay is a goat's-milk cheese made in the form of a truncated cone. The deep blue color of its edible skin comes from the cheese being dusted with vine wood ash. The skin is firm; the interior, soft. Mild in flavor, with a strong goat's-milk aroma, Valençay is similar to Levroux. Valençay is also called Pyramide, for its shape.

WEISSLACKER (VIIS-lahk-er) *Gm.* See Bierkäse.

WENSLEYDALE, *Br.* Wensleydale, originally made in monasteries and farmhouses in Yorkshire, comes in two versions. When young it is fresh and quite similar to Caerphilly, having a slight flavor of buttermilk. The second type of Wensleydale, rarely seen, is a rich double crème blue cheese that rivals Stilton. In fact, some consider blue Wensleydale to be the best of the blues. It is creamy white to pale yellow marbled with blue. Its rich creamy flavor is more delicate than that of Stilton. This rare blue is particularly regarded for its aftertaste. Wensleydale traces its history back to the abbeys of Jervaulx and Fountains, where it is supposed to have been made by the Cistercian monks from an original Norman recipe. When the monasteries were abolished by Henry VIII, the recipe was passed on to the farmers' wives. In those days it was made from sheep's or goat's milk, but since about the seventeenth century, cows have supplied the milk for this cheese.

Don't Ask Your Sommelier

Ordering wine in restaurants can be a tricky bit of business, although it shouldn't be. And the wine service has been known to degenerate into a mystic ritual which neither the waiter nor the diner understands. Here are a few tips on the ordering and serving of wine in restaurants that should shed some light on the subject as well as to increase the enjoyment of dining out.

1. The first thing to keep in mind is that you are the customer, and the customer, remember, is always right. This means that if you order beef and want a white wine, or fish with a red wine, or red wine chilled, or white wine at room temperature, then you shouldn't be hesitant to say so in ordering the wine.

You are, or should be, interested in your own and your companions' pleasure and satisfaction, and not concerned with impressing or gaining the approval of the wine steward, sommelier, or waiter who takes your wine order. Don't allow yourself to be intimidated by a wine steward who isn't sophisticated enough to realize that having wine with your meal should be a pleasure, not a test of how well one has learned the "rules." Order and drink what you like with what you want to eat.

There's no reason, of course, why you shouldn't be open to a reasonable suggestion from the wine steward or sommelier, or even ask his advice. A professional wine steward should know the restaurant's cellar and can often offer valuable information to help you make your choice.

If you would like his assistance, you might tell him the approximate price you want to pay, the style of wine you like, and what dish you plan to order. He can then offer some suggestions, including perhaps some wines that don't appear on the wine list.

2. The wine should be ordered at the same time as the dinner, or even before. This will allow time for the wine to be chilled if it requires chilling, or to breathe if it needs air.

Sparkling wines, whites, and rosés are virtually always served chilled. But a light red wine, such as a Beaujolais or a Bardolino, can also benefit from a little time in the ice bucket. Especially a wine with high acidity, as the chill seems to cut down on the acid.

Opening a bottle to give the contents time to breathe before drinking it is, for young wines with a lot of tannin, to give them time to soften with air; and for big wines with complexities, to allow them to develop through contact with the air. There is disagreement among experts over whether or not wine benefits from the bottle being opened in advance and the wine allowed to breathe before it is poured.

3. Don't shun carafe wines. They're worth inquiring about. Ask which wine it is that the restaurant is serving as the house wine. You will sometimes get a pleasant surprise.

4. If you are ordering a fish course and a meat course, but want only one bottle of wine, you might order a half-bottle of white and a half-bottle of red Another alternative would be to order a glass or two of white and again of red.

5. The wine should be brought to the table, unopened, for your inspection well before the food is served. You should check the label to be sure you are getting the wine you ordered. It is proper to refuse it if it isn't exactly the wine you ordered, which means the producer, shipper, and vintage should be the

same as on the wine list. If not, you are within your rights to refuse it—even if it was already opened (which it should not have been) before being shown to you.

6. Some of the ritual performed in restaurants in serving wine is strictly for show. Do not let this ritual intimidate you if you're not quite sure what to make of some of it.

The baskets used in many restaurants to serve red wine rarely serve any useful purpose. This bin basket was designed to carry an old bottle from the cellar bin to the decanting table or dinner table at an angle so that the sediment in the bottle wouldn't be stirred up into the wine. Since most wines served in restaurants have no sediment, there is nothing to be gained by using the basket for them.

It only makes it more difficult for the wine to be opened without being spilled. That's why you often observe the waiter take the bottle out of the basket, stand it up to pull the cork, then tuck it back into the basket for pouring. Refrain from chuckling—it probably wasn't his idea to use the silly basket. But feel free to ask him to take it away and stand up the bottle, especially if there's not much room on your table.

Sometimes when the wine is opened, the cork will be offered to you or put in front of you for your inspection. The cork will provide you with very little clue as to the wine's drinkability—ignore it.

It may happen that the sommelier will pour himself a little of your wine to taste. This is okay; that is, in some restaurants it is considered part of his job to make sure the wine is not bad before pouring you any. This way your tastebuds aren't assaulted by the "off" taste of a bad wine. This seems to be done more often when the wine in question is an old bottle, where the chances, of course, are greater of its having gone off. This makes your tasting it again rather superfluous. However, if it turns out that it is a bad bottle after all, you can still refuse it.

7. A small amount of wine should be poured into your glass. Check the clarity of the wine. If it is cloudy or hazy, reject it; it has been mishandled. If it is clear, sample it. A young wine can simply be tasted to determine that it isn't bad. An older, more expensive wine should be sniffed (swirling the wine in the glass will increase the bouquet) first and then tasted.

There are really two things to check for in sampling the wine. Is it bad? If so, send it back. And, is it being served at the right temperature? If it is to be served chilled, and is too warm or too cold, ask the wine steward to wait awhile before pouring the wine to give it time to reach the desired temperature.

The only proper reason to return a bottle after sampling it is if it is a bad bottle. It is not proper to return a wine because you don't like it. If the wine is corked (smells like a musty cork), oxidized (smells like Sherry or Madeira rather than wine, and has a bitter taste), or bad in some other way, refuse it. But if you simply don't like it, keep it; you ordered it. A restaurant can't afford to have bottles of wine opened and sent back because the customer doesn't happen to like them. But, by all means, if the wine is really "off," say so and send it back.

The chances of getting a bad bottle in a restaurant are actually not very great. It happens, but rarely.

8. The wine glass should be filled only halfway. There are a couple of reasons for this. First, it allows the aroma or bouquet of the wine to develop a little in the glass. And, in the case of chilled wines, they don't warm up as fast, as they don't sit in the glass as long; you get a cool refill from the chilled bottle for each half-glassful

Wine-Food Affinities

Though tastes in wine and food are an individual thing, varying from person to person, there are certain flavors which have been found to go together very well and most people, or at least many people, will appreciate these combinations of flavors. Chablis and oysters are a classic example.

But not everyone will agree with some combinations of wine and food, and if they don't, they should quite rightly ignore them and come up with a combination that is more to their taste.

The following wine and food affinities are offered as a guide, not a set of rules. Nobody can tell you what you will like, or worse yet, what you *should* like. It's enough to make you lose your appetite!

Go by your own taste; nobody knows what you like as well as you do. Indulge your fancy. The only rule here is your pleasure. So if you enjoy a sweet wine with your fish appetizer—enjoy it. And don't be intimidated by the grimaces of your dining companions grabbing at their midsections and rolling their eyes. Stand firm and offer this toast with your offending wine, *"Chacun à son goût"* (to each his own).

But if you are looking for suggestions, here they are—accept them or reject them or use them as a point of departure to come up with your own ideas, as it suits you.

Before the Meal

The best aperitif to sip before a fine meal is a drink that will whet your appetite and heighten your sensitivity to the pleasures to follow. Spirits, or hard liquor, being high in alcohol, have the tendency to dull your senses, just the opposite of the desired effect. Any of the following makes a good before-dinner drink:

Aperitif
Fortified Wine
Dry Sparkling Wine
Light, Dry White Wine

APERITIF
Cynar
dry vermouth
Lillet
Dubonnet
Raphael

FORTIFIED WINE
Spain: Sherry, Fino or Amontillado
Montilla, Fino or Amontillado
Manzanilla

Portugal: Madeira Sercial

France: Rasteau Vins Doux Naturel
Chateau Chalon

Italy: dry Marsala

California: Muscat de Frontignan

DRY SPARKLING WINE
California: au naturel or brut "Champagne"

France: brut Champagne
Seyssel mousseux

Vouvray mousseux
Saint-Péray mousseux

Germany: dry Sekt

New York: brut sparkling wine

LIGHT, DRY WHITE WINE
California: Riesling
           Sylvaner
           Muscat Alexandria
           Fume Blanc
           Sauvignon Blanc

France: Alsatian Riesling
       Alsatian Sylvaner
       Mâcon or Mâcon Villages
       Beaujolais blanc
       Vouvray
       Sancerre
       Pouilly-Fumé
       Muscadet
       Côtes du Rhône or Côtes du Rhône Villages blanc
       Graves or Graves Supérieur
       Entre-Deux-Mers

Germany: Scharzhofberger
        Bernkasteler Riesling
        Wehlener Sonnenuhr
        Kreuznacher
        Schloss Böckelheimer

Hors d'Oeuvre, Appetizers

FISH DISHES

dry white wine, crisp or fruity
sparkling brut

MEAT DISHES
light red wine

COMBINATION DISHES
sparkling brut
rosé wine

FISH APPETIZERS
(dry white wine, crisp or fruity)

California: Riesling
            Sylvaner
            Muscat Alexandria
            Fume Blanc
            Sauvignon Blanc

France: Alsatian Riesling
        Alsatian Sylvaner
        Mâcon or Mâcon-Villages
        Beaujolais blanc
        Vouvray
        Sancerre
        Pouilly-Fumé
        Muscadet
        Côtes du Rhône or Côtes du Rhône Vil-
            lages blanc
        Graves or Graves Supérieur
        Entre-Deux-Mers
        Chablis
        Meursault
        Puligny-Montrachet
        Chassagne-Montrachet

Germany: Scharzhofberger

Bernkasteler Riesling
Wehlener Sonnenuhr
Kreuznacher
Schloss Böckelheimer
Johannisberger Riesling
Rudesheimer Rosengarten
Eltviller Sonnenberg
Rauenthaler Baiken
Steinberger
Marcobrunner

New York: Johannisberg Riesling
(sparkling brut)

California: au naturel or brut "Champagne"

France: brut Champagne
Seyssel mousseux
Vouvray mousseux
Saint-Péray mousseux

Germany: dry Sekt

New York: brut sparkling wine

MEAT APPETIZERS
(light red wine)

California: Gamay or Gamay Beaujolais
Zinfandel
Pinot Noir

New York: Pinot Noir

France: Beaujolais, Beaujolais Villages, or Beaujolais Supérieur
Bordeaux or Bordeaux Supérieur

Côtes du Rhône or Côtes du Rhône
    Villages
Médoc
Haut-Médoc
Saumur-Champigny
Bourgueil
Chinon

Spain: young Rioja

Italy: Bardolino
      Valpolicella

COMBINATION APPETIZERS
(sparkling brut)

California: au naturel or brut "Champagne"

France: brut Champagne
      Seyssel mousseux
      Vouvray mousseux
      Saint-Péray mousseux

Germany: dry Sekt

New York: brut sparkling wine

(rosé wine)

California: Grenache
      Zinfandel
      Cabernet

France: Tavel
      Lirac
      Côtes de Provence
      Rosé d'Anjou

Germany: Weissherbst

Seafood—Fish and Shellfish

Freshwater Fish:
  light white wine, fruity or dry

Saltwater Fish, delicate flavor:
  light white wine, fruity or dry

Saltwater Fish, full flavor:
  dry, crisp white wine

Shellfish:
  dry, crisp white wine
  dry sparkling wine

Seafood in a Sauce:
  wine depends on the sauce

FRESHWATER FISH AND SALTWATER FISH, DELICATE FLAVOR
(light white wine, fruity or dry)

California: Riesling
            Sylvaner
            dry Chenin Blanc
            Fume Blanc
            Sauvignon Blanc

New York: Johannisberg Riesling

France: Château Grillet
        Condrieu
        Alsatian Riesling
        Alsatian Sylvaner

Mâcon or Mâcon Villages
Beaujolais blanc
Vouvray
Sancerre
Pouilly-Fumé
Muscadet
Côtes du Rhône or Côtes du Rhône Vil-
    lages blanc
Graves or Graves Supérieur
Entre-Deux-Mers
Chablis
Meursault
Puligny-Montrachet
Chassagne-Montrachet

Germany: Scharzhofberger
Bernkasteler Riesling
Wehlener Sonnenuhr
Kreuznacher
Schloss Böckelheimer
Johannisberger Riesling
Rudesheimer Rosengarten
Eltviller Sonnenberg
Rauenthaler Baiken
Steinberger
Marcobrunner

SALT-WATER FISH, FULL-FLAVOR OR SHELLFISH
(dry, crisp white wine)

California: Emerald Riesling
Pinot Chardonnay
Pinot Blanc

New York: Pinot Chardonnay

France: Condrieu
Chablis
Muscadet
Hermitage blanc
Crozes-Hermitage blanc
Saint-Joseph blanc
Lirac blanc
Châteauneuf-du-Pape blanc
Alsatian Riesling
Alsatian Sylvaner

SHELLFISH
(dry sparkling wine)

California: au naturel or brut
"Champagne"

New York: brut sparkling wine

France: brut Champagne
Seyssel mousseux
Vouvray mousseux
Saint-Péray mousseux

Germany: dry Sekt

Sausages and Cold Meats

Sausages:
light red wine

Cold White Meats:
light, fruity white wine

Cold Red Meats:
light to medium-bodied red wine

SAUSAGES
  (light red wine)

  California: Zinfandel
            Gamay
            Pinot Noir
            Red Table Wine

  New York: Pinot Noir
            Red Wine
            Gamay

  France: Beaujolais
          Saumur-Champigny
          Bourgueil
          Chinon

  Spain: young Rioja

COLD WHITE MEATS
  (light fruity white wine)

  California: Pinot Blanc
            Sylvaner
            Grey Riesling
            White Table Wine
            Emerald Riesling

  New York: White Wine
            Johannisberg Riesling

  France: Sylvaner
          Mâcon blanc
          Beaujolais blanc
          Côtes du Rhône blanc
          Entre-Deux-Mers
          Muscadet
          Vouvray

Pouilly-Fumé
Saint-Veran

COLD RED MEATS
(light to medium-bodied red wine)

California: Zinfandel
         Pinot Noir
         Cabernet Sauvignon

New York: Cabernet Sauvignon

France: Bordeaux
        Médoc
        Côtes du Rhône
        Burgundy

Pasta

Generally, the sauce determines the wine
  Light or Creamy Sauce:
    light red wine

  Rich Sauce:
    full red wine

  Spicy Sauce:
    robust red wine

  Seafood Sauce, spicy:
    spicy white wine

  Seafood Sauce, mild:
    full-bodied white wine

LIGHT OR CREAMY SAUCE
(light red wine)

California: Gamay or Gamay Beaujolais
Zinfandel
Pinot Noir

New York: Pinot Noir

France: Beaujolais, Beaujolais Villages, or Beaujolais Supérieur
Bordeaux or Bordeaux Supérieur
Côtes du Rhône or Côtes du Rhône Villages
Médoc
Haut-Médoc
Saumur-Champigny
Bourgueil
Chinon

Spain: young Rioja

Italy: Bardolino
Valpolicella

RICH SAUCE
(full red wine)

California: Zinfandel
Cabernet Sauvignon
Petite Syrah
Carignane
Grenache

France: Côtes du Rhône, Côtes du Rhône Villages
Crozes-Hermitage
Saint-Joseph
Cornas

        Gigondas
        Saint-Emilion
        Pomerol
        Burgundy

Spain: Rioja

Italy: Gattinara
      Spanna

SPICY SAUCE
(robust red wine)

California: Barbera
          Petite Syrah
          Alicante Bouschet
          Carignane

France: Châteauneuf-du-Pape
       Gigondas
       Hermitage

Italy: Barbaresco
      Amarone

SEAFOOD SAUCE, SPICY
(spicy white wine)

California: Gewurztraminer
          Muscat Alexandria

New York: Gewurztraminer
        Pinot Gris

France: Gewürztraminer
       Tokay d'Alsace

SEAFOOD SAUCE, MILD
(full-bodied white wine)

California: Pinot Chardonnay
            Pinot Blanc
            Fume Blanc

New York: Pinot Chardonnay
           Johannisberg Riesling

France: Alsatian Sylvaner
        Alsatian Riesling
        Graves or Graves Supérieur
        Crozes-Hermitage blanc
        Saint-Joseph blanc
        Côtes du Rhône or Côtes du Rhône Vil-
           lages blanc
        Mâcon or Mâcon Villages

Poultry and Wild Fowl

Chicken or Capon:
  dry white wine
  light red wine

Turkey:
  full white wine
  medium red wine

Duck or Goose:
  full red wine

Wild or Well-seasoned Fowl:
  robust red wine

CHICKEN OR CAPON
(dry white wine)

California: Riesling
Sylvaner
Muscat Alexandria
Fume Blanc
Sauvignon Blanc

France: Riesling
Sylvaner
Mâcon or Mâcon Villages
Beaujolais blanc
Vouvray
Sancerre
Pouilly-Fumé
Condrieu
Côtes du Rhône or Côtes du Rhône Villages blanc
Graves or Graves Supérieur
Entre-Deux-Mers
Château Grillet
Meursault
Puligny-Montrachet
Chassagne-Montrachet

Germany: Scharzhofberger
Bernkasteler Riesling
Wehlener Sonnenuhr
Kreuznacher
Schloss Böckelheimer
Johannisberger Riesling
Rüdesheimer Rosengarten
Eltviller Sonnenberg
Rauenthaler Baiken
Marcobrunner
Steinberger

New York: Johannisberg Riesling

(light red wine)

California: Gamay or Gamay Beaujolais
          Zinfandel
          Pinot Noir

New York: Pinot Noir

France: Beaujolais, Beaujolais Villages, or Beau-
          jolais Supérieur
          Bordeaux or Bordeaux Supérieur
          Côtes du Rhône or Côtes du Rhône
          Villages
          Médoc
          Haut-Médoc
          Saumur-Champigny
          Bourgueil
          Chinon

Spain: young Rioja

Italy: Bardolino
     Valpolicella

TURKEY
(full white wine)

California: Pinot Chardonnay
          Pinot Blanc
          Fume Blanc

New York: Pinot Chardonnay
          Johannisberg Riesling

France: Sylvaner
         Riesling
         Graves or Graves Supérieur

Crozes-Hermitage blanc
Saint-Joseph blanc
Côtes du Rhône or Côtes du Rhône Villages blanc
Mâcon or Mâcon Villages
Château Grillet
Châteauneuf-du-Pape blanc

(medium red wine)

California: Zinfandel
Cabernet Sauvignon
Carignane
Petite Syrah

France: Pomerol
Saint-Emilion
Haut-Médoc
Saint-Joseph
Crozes-Hermitage
Côtes du Rhône, Côtes du Rhône Villages
Nuits-Saint-Georges
Vosne-Romanée
Gevrey-Chambertin
Morey-Saint-Denis
Aloxe-Corton

Spain: Rioja

Italy: Spanna

DUCK OR GOOSE
(full red wine)

California: Zinfandel
Cabernet Sauvignon

France: Burgundy
   Pomerol
   Saint-Emilion
   Côtes du Rhône or Côtes du Rhône
    Villages
   Saint-Joseph
   Crozes-Hermitage
   Côte Rôtie

Italy: Spanna
   Gattinara

WILD OR WELL-SEASONED FOWL
(robust red wine)

California: Petite Syrah
    Zinfandel
    Alicante Bouschet
    Cabernet Sauvignon

France: Hermitage
   Côte Rôtie
   Châteauneuf-du-Pape
   Gigondas
   Saint-Emilion
   Burgundy
   Corton
   Chambertin
   Nuits-Saint-Georges
   Romanée-Conti
   Musigny

Italy: Sassella
   Gattinara
   Spanna

White Meats—Veal and Pork

Medium-bodied White Wine
Light to Medium Red Wine

Highly seasoned dishes call for a full red wine.

MEDIUM-BODIED WHITE WINE
California: Pinot Chardonnay
          Pinot Blanc
          Riesling
          Sylvaner
          Muscat Alexandria

New York: Johannisberg Riesling
          Chardonnay

France: Corton-Charlemagne
        Meursault
        Pouilly-Fuissé
        Saint-Veran
        Mâcon blanc
        Côtes du Rhône or Côtes du Rhône Villages blanc
        Saint-Joseph blanc
        Pouilly-Fumé
        Sancerre
        Vouvray
        Riesling
        Sylvaner
        Châteauneuf-du-Pape blanc

LIGHT TO MEDIUM RED WINE
California: Grenache
          Zinfandel
          Pinot Noir

                        Cabernet Sauvignon
                        Merlot

New York: Gamay
           Pinot Noir

France: Beaujolais, Beaujolais Villages, Beaujolais
              Supérieur
           Saumur-Champigny
           Bordeaux or Bordeaux Supérieur
           Côtes du Rhône or Côtes du Rhône
              Villages
           Médoc
           Haut-Médoc
           Bourgueil
           Chinon
           Aloxe-Corton

Spain: Rioja

FULL RED WINE

California: Zinfandel
            Cabernet Sauvignon
            Petite Syrah
            Carignane
            Grenache
France: Crozes-Hermitage
           Saint-Joseph
           Côtes du Rhône, Côtes du Rhône Villages
           Côte Rôtie
           Cornas
           Gigondas
           Saint-Emilion
           Pomerol
           Burgundy

Spain: Rioja

Italy: Gattinara
       Spanna

Red Meat—Beef and Lamb

Steaks, Chops, or Roast Beef:
   medium to full-bodied red wine

Stews, Braised and Boiled Meat:
   full, common red wine

Pot Roasted Meat:
   full or robust red wine

STEAKS, CHOPS, OR ROAST BEEF
   (medium to full-bodied red wine)

California: Cabernet Sauvignon
            Zinfandel
            Merlot

New York: Cabernet Sauvignon

France: Bordeaux
        Haut-Médoc
        Graves
        Saint-Joseph
        Crozes-Hermitage
        Côtes du Rhône or Côtes du Rhône
           Villages
        Côte Rôtie
        Burgundy

STEWS, BRAISED OR BOILED MEAT
(full, common red wine)

California: Barbera
            Zinfandel
            Petite Syrah
            Alicante Bouschet
            Carignane

France: Côtes du Rhône or Côtes du Rhône
        Villages
        Saint-Emilion
        Pomerol
        Burgundy

POT ROASTED MEAT
(full or robust red wine)

California: Petite Syrah
            Zinfandel
            Alicante Bouschet
            Carignane

France: Côtes du Rhône or Côtes du Rhône
        Villages
        Châteauneuf-du-Pape
        Gigondas
        Cornas
        Hermitage
        Côte Rôtie
        Saint-Emilion
        Pomerol

Spain: Rioja

Game

Full, robust red wine

France: Pomerol
       Saint-Emilion
       Hermitage
       Côte Rôtie
       Gigondas
       Châteauneuf-du-Pape
       Burgundy

Spain: Rioja

Italy: Gattinara
     Spanna

California: Cabernet Sauvignon
          Petite Syrah
          Zinfandel
          Alicante Bouschet
          Barbera

Cheese

Mild Cheeses:
   medium-bodied white wine
   light red wine

Medium to Strong Cheeses:
   medium to full-bodied red wine

Pungent Cheeses:
   robust red wine

Blue or Marbled Cheeses:
   robust red wine
   sweet white wine

Goat Cheeses:
   dry white wine

MILD CHEESES
   (medium-bodied white wine)

California: Pinot Chardonnay
            Pinot Blanc
            Fume Blanc
            Muscat Alexandria

New York: Chardonnay

France: Corton-Charlemagne
        Châteauneuf-du-Pape blanc
        Pouilly-Fumé
        Saint-Veran
        Mâcon blanc
        Côtes du Rhône or Côtes du Rhône Villages blanc
        Graves or Graves Supérieur
        Château Grillet
        Sancerre
        Vouvray
        Saint-Joseph blanc

   (light red wine)

California: Gamay or Gamay Beaujolais
            Zinfandel
            Pinot Noir

New York: Pinot Noir
                Gamay

France: Beaujolais, Beaujolais Villages, Beaujolais
                Supérieur
                Bourgueil
                Chinon
                Côtes du Rhône or Côtes du Rhône Vil-
                lages
                Saumur-Champigny
                Médoc
                Haut-Médoc
                Bordeaux or Bordeaux Supérieur

Italy: Bardolino
           Valpolicella

MEDIUM TO STRONG CHEESES
(medium to full-bodied red wine)

California: Zinfandel
                  Cabernet Sauvignon
                  Merlot
                  Petite Syrah

New York: Cabernet Sauvignon
                Pinot Noir

France: Bordeaux
                Haut-Médoc
                Graves
                Pomerol
                Saint-Emilion
                Côtes du Rhône or Côtes du Rhône
                Villages

Saint-Joseph
Crozes-Hermitage
Côte Rôtie
Hermitage
Aloxe-Corton
Gevrey-Chambertin
Vosne-Romanée
Morey-Saint-Denis

Italy: Spanna
Gattinara

BLUE OR MARBLED, OR PUNGENT CHEESES
(robust red wine)

California: Petite Syrah
Zinfandel
Cabernet Sauvignon
Alicante Bouschet

France: Hermitage
Côte Rôtie
Châteauneuf-du-Pape
Gigondas
Saint-Emilion
Corton
Chambertin
Romanée-Conti
Nuits-Saint-George
Pomerol

Italy: Amarone
Gattinara

BLUE OR MARBLED CHEESES
(sweet white wine)

France: Sauternes
  Château d'Yquem
  Château Climens
  Château Coutet
  Barsac

Italy: Vin Santo

Germany: Beerenauslese

GOAT CHEESES
  (dry white wine)

California: Emerald Riesling
  Pinot Chardonnay
  Pinot Blanc

New York: Pinot Chardonnay
  Johannisberg Riesling

France: Chablis
  Muscadet
  Hermitage blanc
  Crozes-Hermitage blanc
  Condrieu
  Saint-Joseph blanc
  Lirac blanc
  Châteauneuf-du-Pape blanc
  Alsatian Riesling
  Alsatian Sylvaner

Fruits, Desserts and Nuts

Fruits and other types of dessert (except ice cream—

it has been our experience that no wine really goes with ice cream; for this, try a liqueur):

Sweet Wine

Nuts:
Sweet Fortified Wine

FRUITS AND DESSERTS
(Sweet Wine)

California: Moscato d'Angelo
Muscat de Frontignan
Angelica

New York: Muscat Ottonel

France: Sauternes
Barsac
Beaumes-de-Venise Vin Doux Naturel
Rasteau Vin Doux Naturel
Clos Quarts de Chaume
Vouvray Moelleux

Germany: Auslese
Beerenauslese

Hungary: Tokaji

Portugal: Port

Spain: Oloroso
Cream Sherry or Montilla

NUTS
(Sweet Fortified Wine)
California: Angelica

France: Beaumes-de-Venise Vin Doux Naturel
        Rasteau Vin Doux Naturel

Portugal: Port (with walnuts)

Spain: Oloroso, Sherry or Montilla

Digestif

France: Cognac
       Armagnac
       Chartreuse
       Benedictine

Italy: Cynar
     Fernet Branca

Cross-Reference

Cheese

Käse
Formaggio
Fromage
Queso
(see) Carrozza, Mozzarella in
     Croque Monsieur
     Crostini alla Provatura
     Fondue
     Fonduta
     Plateau de Fromage
     Quiche
     Raclette
     Rarebit
     Romana, Crostini alla
     Romana, Spiedini alla

Eggs

Eier
Huevos
Oeufs
Uovo
(see) Affogati
     Agnès Sorel
     Benedette
     Benedict
     Fines Herbes, aux
     Pavese, Zuppa alla

Pipérade
Shirred Eggs
Soufflé
Spanish Omelette
Tortilla
Western Omelette

Game

Caccia
Caza
Gibier
Selvaggina
Wild (fleisch)
(see) Cumberland Sauce
      Grand Veneur
      Saint-Hubert

HARE
Hase
Lepre
Liebre
Lièvre
(see) Agrodolce, in
      Hasenpfeffer
      Jugged Hare

PARTRIDGE
Perdiz
Perdreau, Perdrix
Pernice
Rebhuhn

PHEASANT
Fagiano
Faisan

Faisán
Fasan
(see) Souvaroff, Souvarov

PIGEON
Palombe
Paloma
Piccione
Pichón
Pigeon, Pigeonneau
Squab
Taube

QUAIL
Caille
Codorniz
Quaglie
Wachtel

RABBIT
Conejo
Coniglio
Kaninchen
Lapereau, Lapin
(see) Agrodolce, in

VENISON
Cervo
Chevreuil
Hirsch
Reh
Venado
Venaison
(see) Cuissot
      Grand Veneur

Meat

Carne
Fleisch
Viande
(see) Arrosto, Arrostito
    Bollito Misto
    Bonne Femme
    Bouquetière
    Braciola, Braciolette
    Brasciole
    Carbonnade
    Carré
    Cassoulet
    Chaud-Froid
    Chou (Vert) Farci
    Choucroute Alsacienne
    Choucroute Garni
    Choucroute Strasbourgeoise
    Costa, Costata
    Costoletta
    Côte
    Côtelette
    Cotoletta
    Daube
    Émincé
    Épaule
    Escalope
    Filetto
    Fricandeau
    Fricassée
    Goulash
    Grasso, di
    Hochepoche, Hochepot
    Kabobs, Kebabs
    Königsberger Klops

Longe
Marmite, Petite
Mascotte, Mascotti
Medaglione
Médaillon
Mirabeau
Mixed Grill
Nivernaise
Noisettes
Noix
Normande
Paella
Paupiettes
Paysanne
Polpette, Polpettine
Polpettone
Pot-au-Feu
Potée
Rack
Rissoles
Rollatine
Rôti
Saddle
Sainte-Menehould
Schlachtplatte
Selle
Stufatino, Stufato

BEEF
  Bifteck
  Bistec
  Bistecca, Bistecche
  Boeuf
  Bue
  Buey
  Manzo
  Ochsen (fleisch)

Rind (fleisch)
Vaca (Carne de)
(see) Alouettes sans Tête
    Beefsteak and Kidney Pudding
    Bifteck
    Bistecca, Bistecche
    Bistecchina
    Bourguignonne
    Bresaola
    Carbonade
    Carpaccio
    Châteaubriand, Châteaubriant
    Cheval, Bifteck à
    Cheval, Hamburger à
    Coda di Bue
    Daube
    Diane, Steak
    Entrecôte
    Estoufade, Estouffade
    Filetto
    Fiorentina, Bistecca alla
    Fondue Bourguignonne
    Goulash
    Hochepoche, Hochepot
    Mignon, Filet
    Mignonettes
    Minute Steak
    Miroton de Boeuf
    Mode, Boeuf à la
    Oiseaux sans Tête
    Paillard
    Périgourdine, Filet de Boeuf en Croûte
    Poivre, Steak au
    Queue de Boeuf
    Rouladen
    Salisbury Steak
    Sauerbraten

Shashlik
Stracotto
Stroganoff, Stroganov
Tartare
Tournedos
Uccelletti
Wellington, Beef or Steak

HAM
Bayonne, Jambon de
Jambon
Jamón
Prosciutto
Schinken

LAMB
Abbacchio
Agneau
Agneau de Lait
Agnello
Cordero
Lamm (fleisch)
Ternasco
(see) Blanquette
Cacciatore, Abbacchio alla
Carré
Dolmas
French Lamb Chops
Gigot
Irish Stew
Kabobs, Kebabs
Moussaka
Navarin
Noisettes
Persillé
Pieds
Rack

Sainte-Menehould
Shashlik
Trotters

MUTTON
Carnero
Castrato
Hammel (fleisch)
Montone
Mouton
Oveja
Schöpsen (fleisch)
(see) list under Lamb

PORK
Cerdo
Cochon
Cochinillo
Lechón, Lechoncillo
Maiale
Porc
Porcelet
Porcellino
Porchetta
Porco
Schweine (fleisch)
Spanferkel
Tostón
(see) Arista
    Canadian Bacon
    Cochon de Lait
    Fiorentina, Arista
    Kasseler Rippchen or Rippenspeer
    Pieds
    Porchetta
    Potée

Rillettes
Roulade
Sainte-Menehould
Trotters

SAUSAGES
Salame, Salami
Salchichas
Salsiccie
Saucisses
Saucissons
Würst, Würstchen
(see) Choucroûte Alsacienne
Choucroûte Garnie
Choucroûte Strasbourgeoise
Lyonnaise, Saucissons
Peperoni
Rosette

VEAL
Kalb (fleisch)
Ternera
Veau
Vitello
Vitellone
(see) Alouettes sans Tête
Blanquette
Bolognese
Cordon Bleu
Costoletta
Côtelette
Cotoletta
Cuisseau
Fricandeau
Grenadin
Holstein
Involtini

Magenta
Marengo
Marsala
Milanese
Normande
Oiseaux sans Tête
Orloff
Ossi Buchi, Ossobuco
Paillard
Parmigiana
Paupiettes
Piccata
Rollatine
Roulade
Sainte-Menehould
Saltimbocca
Scaloppine
Schnitzel
Suprême
Tonnato, Vitello
Uccelletti
Valdostana
Veal Birds

Poultry

Aves
Geflügel
Pollame
Volaille
(see) Ailerons
Ballotine
Bonne Femme
Cassoulet
Chaud-Froid
Croquettes

Demi-Deuil
Galantina, Galantine
Mascotte, Mascotti
Nid, au
Normande
Paysanne
Quenelles
Royale
Souvaroff, Souvarov
Suprême de Volaille

CAPON
Cappone
Chapon
Kapaun

CHICKEN
Coq
Coquelet
Hendel
Henne
Huhn, Hühnchen
Pollastra
Polletti
Pollito
Pollo
Poularde
Poule
Poulet
Poussin
(see) Arrabbiata
Arroz con Pollo
Bolognese
Budino di Pollo
Cacciatore
Coq au Vin

Cordon Bleu
Cuisses
Demi-Deuil
Diavola
Fricassée
Galantina, Galantine
Gumbo
Kiev
King
Marengo
Marmite, Petite
Maryland Chicken
Paella
Parmigiana
Reine
Rollatine
Southern Fried Chicken
Suprême
Valdostana
Waterzooï

DUCK, DUCKLING
Anatra
Anitra
Anadino
Canard
Caneton
Ente, Entchen
Mastente
Pato
(see) Bigarade
Chaud-Froid
Montmorency
Orange
Presse

        Pressed Duck
        Rouennaise

GOOSE
    Gans
    Ganso
    Oca
    Oie

TURKEY
    Dinde, Dindonneau
    Tacchino
    Truthahn
    Truthenne
    Pavo

Seafood

    Fruits de Mer
    Fruta del Mar
    Frutta di Mare
    Meerfutter
    (see) Bouillabaisse
            Brodetto
            Cardinal
            Cioppino
            Duglère
            Fritto Misto di Mare
            Fritto Misto di Pesce
            Gribiche
            Insalata di Mare
            Insalata di Pesce
            Livornese
            Marinara
            Marinière
            Normande

Paella
Tartare, Sauce

FISH
Fische
Pescado
Pesce
Pez
Poisson
(see) Anglaise, Sole
Caviale
Caviar
Chaud-Froid
Colbert
Croquettes
Darne
Dieppoise
Doria
Koulibiac, Kulibiaka
Marguery
Matelote
Meunière
Mugnaia
Orly
Paupiettes
Quenelles
Saint-Germain
Vert-Pré
Walewska
Waterzooï

Frogs' Legs
Froschschenkel
Grenouille, Cuisses de
Rane, Gambe di
Ranas, Piernas de
(see) Provençale, Grenouilles à la

Herring
   Aringa, Aringhe
   Arenque
   Hareng
   Heringe
   (see) Bismarck Herring
        Kippered Herring
        Maatjes Herring
        Matjes Herring
        Rollmops, Rollmöpse

Mackerel
   Caballa
   Escombro
   Makrele
   Maquereau
   Scombro
   Sgombro
   (see) Vin Blanc, Maquereau au

Salmon
   Lachs
   Salmón
   Salmone
   Saumon
   (see) Bellevue, en
        Doria
        Écosse, Saumon d'
        Koulibiac, Kulibiaka

Sole
   Lenguado
   Seezunge
   Sfoglie
   Sogliola
   Sole
   (see) Anglaise

Bonne Femme
Dover Sole
Inglese
Lemon Sole
Mâconnaise
Manche, de la
Marguery
Paupiettes
Suprême
Véronique
Walewska

Trout
Forelle
Trota
Trucha
Truite
(see) Amandes, aux
Amandine
Bleu, au

SHELLFISH
Coquillages
Crostacei
Crustacés
Mariscos
Molluschi
Molluske
Moluscos
Muscheltiere
Schaltiere
(see) Bisque
Cocktail, Seafood
Coquille, en
Coquille de Fruits de Mer
Gribiche
Gumbo

        Half-shell, on the
        Insalata di Mare
        Insalata di Pesce
        Nage
        Posillipo

Clams
    Almejas
    Arselle
    Palourdes
    Praire
    Venusmuschel
    Vongole
    (see) Arreganata
        Casino
        Chablis, au
        Cherrystones
        Little Necks
        Manhattan Style
        New England Style
        Oreganata
        Posillipo
        Reganata
        Zuppa di Vongole

Crab
    Cámbaro
    Cangrejo
    Crabe
    Grancevole
    Granchio
    Krabbe
    (see) Cocktail, Seafood
        Louis
        Moleche
        Moux, Crabes
        Soft-Shell Crabs

Lobster, Rock Lobster
   Aragosta
   Bogavante
   Homard
   Hummer
   Langosta
   Langouste
   (see) Américaine
        Armoricaine
        Bellevue, en
        Cocktail, Seafood
        Fra Diavolo
        Nage
        Newburg
        Thermidor

Mussels
   Cozze
   Mejillones
   Mitili
   Moules
   Muscoli
   Muscheln
   (see) Billi Bi
        Marinière
        Posillipo

Oysters
   Austern
   Huîtres
   Ostras
   Ostriche
   (see) Blue Points
        Cape Cods
        Casino
        Cheval, Huîtres à

Horseback, Angels on
Rockefeller

Scallops
Almejón
Cappa santa
Coquille Saint-Jacques
Kammuschel
Petonchio
Pétoncle
Viera
(see) Bay Scallops
Coquilles Saint-Jacques
Provençale

Shrimp
Camarónes
Crevettes
Gambas
Gamberetti, Gamberi
Garnelen
Prawns
Scampi
(see) Cocktail, Seafood
Scampi
Tapas

Snails
Bovolino
Caracol
Chiocciola
Escargot
Lumaca
Schnecke
(see) Bourguignonne, Escargots à la